HOME IS WHERE HEART IS:

TINY HOUSES, VANS, AND LIVING YOUR BEST LIFE

KRISTINE HUDSON

© 2021 Home is Where Heart Is: Tiny Houses, Vans, and living your best life

All rights reserved. No part of the book may be reproduced in any shape or form without permission from the publisher.

This guide is written from a combination of experience and high-level research. Even though we have done our best to ensure this book is accurate and up to date, there are no guarantees to the accuracy or completeness of the contents herein.

This book has been designed using resources from unsplash.com

ISBN: 978-1-953714-41-1

The best part of any adventure is the special memories you make along the way!

This travel journal will provide you full access to chronicling your journey and adventures through van life. Go to **https://www.kristine-hudson.com/vanlife** to download it for free.

Reviews

Reviews and feedback help improve this book and the author. If you enjoy this book, we would greatly appreciate it if you could take a few moments to share your opinion and post a review on Amazon.

Also by Kristine Hudson

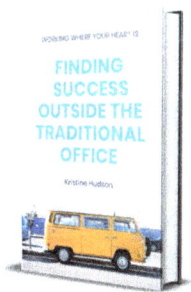

Finding Success Outside The Traditional Office

mybook.to/workfromanywhere

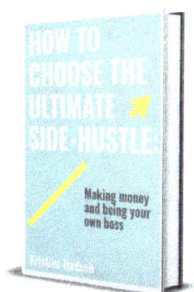

How to Choose the Ultimate Side-hustle

mybook.to/side-hustle

From Wheels to Wellness

mybook.to/Healthinvan

Contents

How to Live the Dream: Things Every Van Lifer Needs to Know — 9

Section 1: Making the Big Decision — 11

Chapter 1: Why Do I Want to Live in a Van? — 12

Chapter 2: The Reality of Van Living - Doing Your Homework — 17

Chapter 3: The Human Element of Van Life- Health and Wealth — 22

Advice from The Road- Part 1 — 26

Section 2: Finding Your New Home — 31

Chapter 1: Considerations for Choosing the Right Vehicle — 31

Chapter 2: So Many Choices! — 37

Chapter 3: Ready-to-Roll, or Ready-to-Rehab? — 44

Chapter 4: Budget Considerations for Creating Your Van — 50

Chapter 5: The Search Process — 56

Advice from the Road- Part 2 — 60

Section 3: Creating and Maintaining a Budget While on the Road — 63

Advice from the Road: Part 3 — 63

Chapter 1: Determining Your Budget — 65

Advice from the Road: Part 4 — 69

Chapter 2: Sticking to It — 71

Chapter 3: Earning Income While on the Move   73

   Advice from the Road: Part 5   74

Section 4: Preparing for Your Trip   77

Chapter 1: Your Utilities   77

Chapter 2: Sleeping Arrangements   78

   Advice from the Road: Part 6   82

Chapter 3: Storage Solutions   82

Chapter 4: Emergency Kit   85

Chapter 5: Food   88

Section 5: Where Are You Going to Go?   93

   Advice from the Road: Part 7   96

Section 6: Staying Happy on the Road   99

Chapter 1: Avoiding Boredom   100

Chapter 2: Homesickness/Loneliness   102

   Advice from the Road: Part 8   103

Chapter 3: Housekeeping   104

In Conclusion   107

Section 7: Helpful Resources for Future Van Dwellers   111

Little Home Big Dreams: The Tiny Home Lifestyle For Beginners — 117

Introduction — 119

Author's Note: How We Fell into Tiny House Living — 125

Chapter 1: Getting Started — 129

    Section 1: What is a Tiny Home? — 130

    Section 2: The goals of living in a tiny home — 134

    Section 3: Challenges of living in a tiny home — 138

Chapter 2: Finding a Tiny Home — 145

    Section 1: Prefabricated tiny houses — 146

    Section 2: Building your own tiny home — 148

    Section 3: Deciding which version is best for you — 152

Chapter 3: Land, Location, and Legal Considerations of Tiny Home Dwelling — 161

    Section 1: Building on a permanent foundation — 162

    Section 2: Considerations for a tiny house on wheels — 166

    Section 3: The Legal Bits — 171

Chapter 4: Settling into a Tiny House — 177

    Section 1: Furniture, Tiny-Style — 179

    Section 2: Appliances and Fixtures — 183

Section 3: Balancing Function and Finishes — 189

Chapter 5: *Mini*-mizing Your Lifestyle — 195

Section 1: Reducing possessions and clutter — 197

Types of Organization Perspectives — 200

Section 2: Keeping your tiny house clean — 206

Section 3: Tiny home dining solutions — 209

Section 4: Tips for children and pets — 214

Conclusion — 221

Resources — 224

Knowledge Base/FAQs — 225

General Assistance — 225

Tiny House Construction — 226

Interior Aspects — 228

Power and Utilities — 229

More Details on Organization Styles and Options — 230

Experiences/Blogs — 231

Communities — 231

HOW TO LIVE THE DREAM:

THINGS EVERY VAN LIFER NEEDS TO KNOW

Kristine Hudson

Section 1: Making the Big Decision

There's a certain romance to the idea of living on the road. Traveling wherever the wind blows. Leaving nothing except footprints. Taking nothing but pictures.

The media is awash with images of attractive, wind-swept people, staring out of their windows at an awe-inspiring vista. Mountains, oceans, and fields so far and wide, you can hardly see the horizon. All these images make van living look like an incredible option. Not only do you get to shed the boring, stale, workaday lifestyle, but you get to wake up wherever you want.

To many, van living is the ultimate goal. It is the dream that just won't go away. While there's tons of material in the media explaining how amazing van life is, there is little to help you prepare for the reality of life on the road.

We'll explore what it takes to hack a nomadic lifestyle in the 21st century, with road tips provided from actual American van dwellers. Throughout this book, you'll find "Advice from the Road," which contains tips, tricks, and details provided by folks who have personally practiced the van lifestyle.

We'll start with all the considerations you'll need to keep in mind before making the decision to follow your wanderlust. We'll also go through the process of choosing your new home, as well as things to consider when creating and utilizing space. Budgeting, as well as managing income and expenditures, is also a huge part of van life. We'll help you get packed and ready to hit the trails, with some tips and tricks for staying happy and learning to find your home on the road.

You might be surprised at how involved the process is, but bear in mind that this is always your adventure. You can ramp up or tame the journey to meet your preferred lifestyle. After all, this is *your* life's dream!

Chapter 1: Why Do I Want to Live in a Van?

Before you start the engine and bid farewell to your friends and family — before you even have an engine to start — you must get in touch with your dream. This may sound a bit New Age, but the reality is that you are about to commit to a very significant lifestyle change by living in a van. Whether you have a regular nine-to-five job that you're sick of, or have been a freewheeling freelancer for years, van living is nothing like what you have experienced to date.

You will not be able to come home. If you have a rough day, you won't be able to "just stay in and order a pizza." The routines that have come to rule your life will no longer exist.

If hearing that makes your heartbeat a little faster, you're not alone. The primary reason people choose van life is because they are sick of having a home and a yard, or an apartment and neighbors. They're tired of commuting to work. They don't want to spend an entire weekend cleaning floors and dusting knick-knacks. They want to live.

If you identify with this, you're on the right track. But here's one important question to ask yourself: By living on the road, what do you hope to achieve? What deep, burning need in your life will van living satisfy, and are you prepared to make a significant number of sacrifices to find that lifestyle?

Let us point out before you start feeling less certain about van living: there are different types of van living experiences.

First, there's the type of Van Lifers who maintain their home and daily lifestyle but use their van as a mobile escape. In previous decades, truly adventurous families had vacation properties, such as beach condos or lakeside cabins. The modern twist on this is to make the holiday home a van, so adventure may take place anywhere you can imagine to drive.

Then there are the semi-permanent nomads. These folks may have a PO Box in a permanent location. They may live full time in the van, but they stay tied to a particular area, whether that be an RV park, long-term campground, or the general vicinity. They may take off for an adventure now and again, but they migrate only around a certain radius.

Lastly, there are the true devotees. These folks plan to see as much as possible and do as much as they can before their time on this planet expires. They hope to never see the same sunset or sunrise — though if they do, they maintain it's purely because they wanted to see that view one more time. These folks don't plan to land on terra firma any time soon and are fully prepared to have all their needs fulfilled by life on the road.

You may fit firmly within one of these categories. You might find yourself somewhere in shades in between. Remember, there is no "wrong way" to organize your dreams. The goal of van life is to fulfill a need you have deep in your soul, and if your soul decides it wants to come home and do a load of laundry, that does not mean you're not accomplishing your dream.

When it comes to van living, there are a few aspects of the lifestyle that tend to be magnets to most people considering the option. Let's explore those in more detail.

The Chance to Live Off-Grid
While "keeping up with the Joneses'" has been part of the American Dream for over a century, there are many who are no longer impressed with this ideal. A larger house might be a great fantasy, but that involves a heftier house payment — which means working more hours. And a bigger house means more "stuff," like furniture and decorations. Owning more means increased upkeep, higher utility bills, taking care of a bigger lawn, etc. For some folks, this sounds less like the American Dream and more like a terrifying nightmare.

A van does not have a mortgage, though you might find yourself making payments on your roaming home — we'll discuss that more later. A van doesn't have utility bills. A van doesn't have an attic to maintain or a basement that floods when it rains. A van doesn't have noisy neighbors. You will do no yard work.

But that doesn't mean it's completely carefree. A van is a mechanical invention, and it can break down. Windows can crack. Tires can blow. You'll need to find new ways of creating power. You will not have running water unless you create that option. If anything breaks, you will have to take care of it, and immediately. While van living does mean you'll be living off the grid, it does not mean you'll live without responsibility.

The Ability to Be Self-Sustaining
Urban and suburban lifestyles require constant connection. You have neighbors. You have coworkers. You have friends. Your social obligations require you to continually connect with these individuals in order to sustain your network and relationships. How much time do you have to yourself?

Traveling the country solo, with just the wind as your copilot may seem like the best way to completely disconnect and shed all these social responsibilities. You have the chance to be alone with your own mind and learn who you are. You can discover how your mind and soul work, and uncover the mystery of who you want to become before your time on this planet draws to a close.

When you work 40-80 hours a week, 52 weeks of the year, you lose the connection with yourself and become the routine that maintains your lifestyle. Being on the road will tear you away from what you've known as life, and guide you to understanding who you really are.

And that means completely upending that routine. What will you do on Saturday mornings, if not going to meet friends for brunch, followed by cleaning the bathroom? When Monday morning arrives, how will you greet the day if you don't have to shower and get ready for work before the sun rises?

For many of us, our lifestyle is determined by what we need to do to keep doing the same thing. When you live on the road, you no longer have to sustain these patterns. While you certainly can continue to work in an office if that's your preference, you won't feel the pressure to work 12-hour days to pay the bills. It certainly won't take you multiple hours to clean the bathroom. Every aspect of your life will be simplified to the most basic needs, rather than creating a level of comfort.

Will you be able to live without guidelines, restrictions, or limitations of someone else? Will you choose instead to learn how to self-sustain, the way humans were intended to live?

The Freedom to Roam
When you no longer live under the demands of someone else's schedule, you have the ability to create your own agenda. This means you can go anywhere you want. You can see what you want to see. Do what you want to do. You don't have to be in the boardroom for a meeting at 3 pm every day. You don't have to take a day off work to wait for the repair technician because the cable isn't working. You have the freedom to dictate your own schedule, and your home has four rubber wheels that are designed to take you anywhere.

This may sound absolutely ideal for many, but it can also cause a bit of anxiety for others. Choice paralysis is real, and some people might have a hard time deciding what to do next. After all, hunting and gathering is no longer a truly viable option in the United States, so following the herds and water sources is not a requirement for survival.

The freedom to roam also means you have to decide where you're going to go. You may be the type of person who has to know where you're going to be on any given day, and that's a hard habit to break. When it is midnight and you're driving through a severe thunderstorm, you might regret not having found a place to park and turn in for the night. After all, though you may shed the responsibilities of suburban life, you'll never get past biological needs!

Even at its most liberating, van life still demands a certain amount of planning and research. While you'll have the ability to go anywhere you want, you still have to acknowledge the practicalities, legalities, and realities that await you.

See the World on Your Own Time
Now that you are no longer living under someone else's agenda, you have to create your own. This doesn't have to be a hard-set "to-do" list of daily chores, but instead, a list of goals and accomplishments you'd like to have under your belt in time.

Before you hit the road, create a list of places you'd like to see, or things you'd like to do. Want to summit El Capitan? Fantastic. Have a burning desire to see the sun rise on the southernmost point of the country? Excellent. Consider themes and key points of interest that really get your blood pumping. Now that you have this freedom, it's time to make the most of it.

Once you are on the road, you truly have the ability to see the world. If you choose to make van living a full-time lifestyle, then this is not a vacation. You do not have to be back in the office in three days' time. You don't need to hire someone to water the plants. If you are going to be a part-time road warrior, however, then you will need to adjust accordingly, which makes having an agenda even more important. After all, the reason you've chosen to live in a van, instead of a tiny house or exotic cave, is because you embrace mobility.

Consider the Alternative
Now that you've really defined why you feel compelled to live in a van, consider the option of not living in a van.

That's right — the time has come to ask yourself why this is so important. One way to make your desires truly transparent is to look at the situation from the flip side.

What if you don't pursue this? What if you just stay home, continue working your job, making sure your knick-knacks don't get dusty? Maybe you go camping every weekend to scratch that wanderlust itch, but you don't go all the way into van living. Would this be something that you would regret?

Living in a van is demanding. Physically, you'll find you have to spend a significant amount of time driving. Your gym routine is likely a thing of the past, too, and you'll have to find ways to feed yourself that don't involve a full-sized kitchen. Emotionally, you will be alone with your thoughts, all day, every day. Are you prepared to keep yourself entertained? Are you comfortable addressing all of the thoughts, hopes, dreams, and emotions that have been ignored while you go with the urban flow? Mentally, you're going to have to prepare for a new set of dangers and challenges, while remaining open to rewards that would never be possible when living in a two bedroom walk-up.

Successful van life is more than just knowing how to set up your bathroom and innovative storage. It is far more than dangling tan legs out the window or watching the sun rise and set in new, amazing places. This is an opportunity to shed not only your electric bill, but every expectation that has ever been made of you and your abilities. You will need to learn a new set of survival skills, and the things that made you feel "comfortable" in a home-dwelling lifestyle will no longer be the same.

In many ways, van living is an entirely new life, and this is a journey that will require dedication and preparation in order to serve you well. You will learn much along the way; in fact, many would argue that you'll learn far more about life when living on the road. However, you have to be prepared to execute those skills and to be ready for a new set of challenges.

Chapter 2: The Reality of Van Living - Doing Your Homework

Before making the decision to commit to van life, it is important that you understand all the challenges and potential hazards that come with the lifestyle. While you have a new and exciting level of freedom, you are going to encounter a new level of responsibility. Not only do you have complete control over where you roam, but you are required to solve every problem that might arise.

This is not to say these problems are too hard to solve. In fact, being prepared before you hit the road will help turn these problems into a variety of inconveniences, rather than taking all the zest out of van living. You will find that one of the key elements to a successful van lifestyle is planning and preparation, which can begin as soon as you start daydreaming about the possibilities.

Let's look at some of the key areas in which you'll need to practice good planning and preparation. This includes: knowing how to keep up with van maintenance, being aware of your equipment, keeping it in good working order, and finding places to park and catch up on rest.

Van Maintenance
Taking care of yourself will be critical on the road, but taking care of your van will be equally important. Therefore, you will need to learn some basic van maintenance.

There are many aspects of vehicle repair and preservation that are relatively simple and can be conducted on nearly any flat service. Being able to check, monitor, and replenish your fluids is a great place to start. Oil, coolant, transmission fluid, brake fluid, and power steering fluid are all things that will need constant observation when you live on the road. They need very little automotive skill to learn where to find the input point, what type to buy, and when to top off your supply.

You may want to invest a little more effort into your overall maintenance skills in order to preserve your overall autonomy. There are two basic facts that apply to any van living situation:
1. A vehicle in motion will require more maintenance, more frequently.
2. Vans require specialized mechanics in many cases. Some vans have a different type of mechanical engineering, and others are

too heavy for a regular repair shop's lift system. In either case, you will not be able to simply roll your van up to any mechanic's shop for basic maintenance.

These two reasons make a compelling case for learning how to do your own basic vehicle care, such as changing oil and oil filters, as well as air filters and fuel filters. While finding a mechanic who can work on your van might be tricky, finding an auto parts store that carries the items you need is far less challenging.

Knowing your vehicle inside and out isn't entirely necessary, especially if you have a particular mechanical ineptitude; however, you will want to become familiar enough with your van to diagnose certain issues. You may want to consider a few automotive classes or online courses. You can also enhance your knowledge or learning process by checking out online videos, which you can bookmark for future reference.

Once you have learned the basic mechanical anatomy and processes of your vehicle, you will want to keep several references in your vehicle at all times. The first is the owner's manual. It can be somewhat tricky to track down owner's manuals, especially if you are purchasing an older vehicle or one that has already gone through several rounds of remodels or rehabs. However, you should be able to find supplemental information online that can provide key information on motors, as well as years, makes, and models of a variety of vehicles.

In addition to the owner's manual, you will want a repair handbook specific to your vehicle type. Understanding the basics in your vehicle could save you hundreds of dollars and days of possible lost time, simply by being able to identify where the problem is.

Lastly, you will need to keep immaculate maintenance records of your own. Not only will this help you track when you need regular preventive care, like oil changes and tire rotations, but can help you record any patterns or trouble areas, such as brakes wearing down too quickly or hoses needing replacing more frequently than you imagined.

As you learn about your vehicle, pay attention to what tools you'll need to fix common repair techniques. Often these tools will be useful for a variety of maintenance in and around the van and will become part of your onboard kit.

Your Key Equipment

While we'll discuss the type of equipment you'll need in your van further in Section 2 and 3, it is important to note that you will also be responsible for the care and maintenance of the equipment within your van.

This can include everything from your cooking surface to your water and power systems, to your most low-tech equipment, such as a cooler or tent.

When living in a van, you do not have the luxury of packing loads of supplies. Instead, you have limited space and thus need to pack only necessary gear, and tools essential for the repair of that gear. For example, instead of packing a main tent and a spare, a better use of space is to pack a tent and a tent repair kit.

You may also be limited as to what you can easily replace. Buying new screens for your windows may seem tempting, but your budget will dictate whether you can do this. Instead, consider learning how to repair the equipment that you will have onboard.

This will likely mean investing in tools and common repair elements, such as tarps, duct tape, twine, and more. As you learn how each piece of equipment in your van works, learn how it can fail to function and what you'll need to have onboard to keep it in good working order. Again, this will save you hundreds of dollars and tons of frustration.

Locations for Landing

At some point in your day, you will need to rest. Your van will also likely thank you for the break. Therefore, you will need to know where, when, and how long you can park your van in a variety of locations. After all, getting a ticket or threatened with towing will put a real damper on your experience... and budget.

Unfortunately, "free parking" is more a thing of the past in inhabited areas. Loiterers and an influx of illegal activity have really put a damper on being able to park and sleep for the night. However, there are some locations in which you'll be able to catch at least a few hours of shut-eye.

Some retail locations — especially stores that supply outdoor activities — still permit adventurers of all kinds a few hours to rest in their parking lots. Before you make assumptions, however, be sure to check with store management to understand the parameters of their offerings. Also, you'll always want to obey posted signage. Sometimes the business does not own the parking lot, so separate rules will apply to those traveling through.

Truck stops and rest areas are other popular spots for a quick rest. Again, there may be time limits on your stay. Always obey posted signs and local ordinances. These will generally be posted in a common area of the rest stop.

Another fantastic resource for free parking is National Land. This refers to land within National Forests or territory that is not otherwise owned or maintained by a private owner. The majority of this land lies west of the Mississippi River, and can be a fantastic opportunity for van people. While these are not paved or maintained sites, and they will not feature luxuries such as even the most remote vault toilet, you can find flat, remote places where you can legally park for free. Once again, there may be limits on how long you can stay in these spots.

Finding spots to park may seem like a game of roulette, but there are actually many resources available to help you hunt down options. (These have been included in the **Resource Guide** at the end of the book.) Van people are, above all, sympathetic to each others' quests and willing to help out whenever possible. Therefore, a wealth of information can be found online or even by talking to others on the road.

Van living does require knowledge and skills, beyond that which you may have at the outset of planning your new lifestyle. However, keep in mind that any lifestyle has a learning curve. When you moved into your house, for example, you probably had to learn where all the light switches were, or how to get the hot water to work. Van living is a very similar experience — you need to learn a new skill set. But once learned, it will help you immeasurably and become part of your daily rituals.

Chapter 3: The Human Element of Van Life- Health and Wealth

Besides requiring a certain amount of mechanical know-how, there are quite a few existential challenges you will encounter on the road, which require mental preparation before you embark on your new mobile lifestyle.

One thing to keep in mind is that you are by and large in control of your overall experience. Everything you have, you make happen. You will no longer have the opportunity to walk over to the neighbor's house to borrow a cup of sugar. You will need to be prepared for everything the road throws at you.

At the same time, do not be bogged down by responsibility. While van living is a totally different type of lifestyle, in time, it will become second nature. Just as you had to figure out life in your first apartment or how to adapt to your first job; you will learn to live in a van. However, be gentle with yourself and allow yourself time to get comfortable with the notion. In the early days, you may question your decision or find yourself unsure of what to do next. This is normal. We all experience growing pains and a learning curve whenever we make huge changes in our lives.

To begin, you can prepare for your new lifestyle before you even purchase your van. Not only can you learn maintenance procedures and parking regulations, but you can prepare yourself for the challenges you'll face as a human as well.

Your Health

In addition to taking care of your van and equipment, you will need to take care of yourself while you are on the road. Not only will your body need to be fed when it is hungry, have access to adequate clean water, and rest when necessary, but you will need regular maintenance as well. Staying in perfect health becomes more complicated when you are on the road. You will be exposed to a new world of germs, and you won't be able to visit your regular doctor if you start feeling under the weather.

There are many things you can do, to ensure your health is always a priority:

1. Pack a first aid kit, including care for multiple types of wounds and injuries. This includes bandages, wraps, antiseptic cream, absorbent pads, athletic wrap and tape, as well as instant ice packs and heat packs.
2. Pack a wellness kit, too. This can include cold medicine, over-the-counter products for pain and fever, topical cream for sprains and strains, throat lozenges, sleep aids, and products for heartburn or upset stomachs.
3. Consider a daily vitamin. Even with a refrigeration system, you won't be able to have full, immediate access to all the fresh fruit and vegetables you had at home, so make sure your body and immune system are fully prepared.
4. If you are on any daily prescriptions, talk to your prescribing physician before you hit the road. You may wish to transfer your prescriptions to a national pharmacy chain and purchase prescriptions in 90-day supplies whenever possible. Often, this will require your doctor's approval. Also share with your doctor where you will be traveling, as some states do not permit non-residents to pick up certain prescriptions. You do not want

to suffer the side effects of missed essential medication while on the road, as that can quickly become serious. Planning ahead with your doctor will ensure you are ahead of the game.
5. Illness will happen. Before you hit the road, consider what your backup plan will be in case you are too sick to drive for several days. Hotels and long-term parking facilities can be expensive but may prove necessary when you are sick. The alternative of driving while you are unable has far greater consequences.
6. Consider your insurance situation, as well. What will happen if you need to go to the hospital, emergency room, or urgent care? In the United States, private insurance is often a requirement to offset very high expenses. What is your plan for carrying insurance during your travels?

Mental Wellness

In addition to your physical well-being, consider your mental health, as well. Being on the road is not always fun! The road will bring more rewards than regrets, but there will be days when you are stationary because of maintenance, sickness, or complacency. There will be days when you "just don't wanna." If you have a "go, go, go" type of plan, there may come a time when you want to "rest, rest, rest." You will need to listen to your mind and body when these days happen because your health is always going to be a huge factor in your overall success on the road.

What will you do when the weather is bad? You might have a day of hiking washed out by unexpected thunderstorms. You may plan to do some maintenance but find yourself unable to do so on a foggy day. Things will not always go as planned, and sometimes the impeding factor is the weather itself. You will likely not want to spend the day confined in your van, which means you'll need to learn how to play along with Mother Nature. Not only will you need a solid weather app, but weather gear, as well. There are certain points in the United States where snow exists year-round. There are also locations where the temperatures can reach over 100 degrees.

Besides being prepared with equipment, make sure you're mentally ready for bad weather, too. If it's going to rain, perhaps you find a local, free museum. If the temperatures are going to be incredibly high, sleep during the day and drive at night to avoid overheating yourself and your van.

Additionally, boredom is real. Finding structure will help you prevent this, but it's going to happen. You might have a daily ritual, but even that will become tedious at times. Even when you find yourself driving to your next adventure, you might find yourself sick of driving and tired of listening to the same old music. This is natural. Don't take boredom as a sign of failure. Instead, pull over and find a new station, podcast, or audiobook. Perhaps you can take some time to catch up on your housekeeping and organization. Maybe you pause and write down how you're feeling. Do a search online for somewhere nearby to take a stroll and clear your thoughts.

When you feel this way at home, what do you do? Most likely, you throw on some television, or call your friends, or find something around the house to occupy your time. You can still do these things on the road, too! It's entirely ok to feel burnt out on driving all the time. Allow yourself downtime, and when you find yourself feeling bored of that, seek out new ways to occupy your time. Consider picking up games and activity books or coloring books. What about journaling? If you're a creator, you can still paint, knit, and craft on the road, or dabble in whatever your preferred media is. Anything you can do to occupy your time can be done in a van, as long as you're willing to change the scale. For example, you won't be able to throw an entire pottery wheel and kiln on your van, but you can grab some modeling clay and play with making tiny creations that will exercise your talent and creativity.

Your Wealth

Despite not having fixed bills, van living can be expensive. Prepare for this now. Before you start budgeting — which we'll discuss in another section — you need to know what types of expenses you can encounter. This includes everything from mechanical breakdowns and flat tires, to daily expenses, like gasoline, food, water, and generator operation. Parking permits cost money, and showering on the road can cost money too (if you don't have a water supply onboard). Every cup of coffee you purchase at a gas station dips into your budget.

If you plan to make a van living your full-time lifestyle, what will you do for income? Many employers offer the opportunity to work remotely, which can be a huge benefit, depending on your profession. This also means you'll likely need to be sure you have a functioning laptop and a reliable Wi-Fi signal. While more and more public locations offer free Wi-Fi, consider if you'll really want to spend every day in a new coffee shop or home improvement store parking lot borrowing signals in order to send in a big report. Instead, you may wish to invest in a web connection amplifier or booster, so that you can run your office right from your van.

You may instead decide to do freelance work on the road. You'll be surrounded by infinite muses, so if you are able to do so, make it happen! You can also run a blog or livestream your journey. Again, this will require a Wi-Fi signal and likely a handful of equipment, so be sure you have a solid plan in place before you set up your van. Having an adequate workspace in your van will definitely increase your professional success.

Van living is incredibly rewarding; however, it does include a bit of adaptation, especially if you've lived a relatively sedentary, domestic life. You may feel like a proverbial fish out of water for some time, but this does not mean you're "doing it wrong." In fact, it means you're finally spreading your wings and finding your groove.

Advice from The Road- Part 1

I hate to be the bearer of bad news, but everything is going to go wrong. Not necessarily all at once, but don't rule that out!

When we hit the road, we started slowly. We started with a two week trip around the vicinity of our home. We wanted to make sure that, no matter what happened, we would be within a reasonable distance of our actual home, so we could "come back" if everything proved to be too much. That included too expensive, too scary, too unpredictable... if at any point we got overwhelmed, we could dart back home and say we had a very nice, short vacation.

Everything went according to plan. We saw the sights, we took the back roads, we gathered loads of amazing photographs and memories. Then, just nine hours away from home, everything went sideways. Huge mechanical breakdown — one of those situations where one thing breaks, and then all the bits and pieces around it start breaking. It was beyond anything we could take care of ourselves because so many things were just falling apart.

Worse yet — we were supposed to be in a wedding at home in just two days!

We had the choice of trying to find someone who could help fix it, or just abandon our van, find a rental car, and figure out how to get the van back later. It took all day, but we were able to find — and get the van to — a mechanic. Even then, it wasn't fixable without ordering parts that would take several days to arrive.

Thankfully, the mechanic was sympathetic to van life. He'd done it himself. Since he couldn't fix it, he came up with a suitable workaround that would get us home. He also recommended that, once we started driving, we not stop except for fuel.

We thought we were home free but still fell prey to the mayhem that can be road life. Even when you think things are going well, it just takes one situation to remind you that "fine" is a temporary state of mind.

Still, there's nothing I'd give up about life on the road. Bad things happen in an apartment. Your car can break down on the way to the office. Your milk will go bad, and your dog will barf in your shoes.

A Van Lifer is someone who can adapt, overcome, and think of creative situations to nearly every problem. Furthermore, they accept that sometimes the solution is "ask an expert." Van Life is a community effort, even if that community is constantly moving in different directions!

Did we get back on the road? Absolutely! We had to spend a bit more time at home than we planned, getting the parts we needed, but that gave us time to learn more about the situation and research solutions for when (not if) it happened again.

Section 2: Finding Your New Home

Being aware of what it takes to successfully live on the road is all well and good, but once you have your mind made up, it's time to find the chariot that will carry you through all of life's adventures.

Again, you might take to the internet to find pictures of vans with white-washed walls, gleaming hardwood floors, tile backsplashes, and even wood-burning stoves. Looks awfully cozy, doesn't it?

While you can make these beautiful images part of your reality, the truth is that it will take a lot of work to get there.

In this section, we'll look at the different things you need to keep in mind when choosing your new vehicle, as well as how to proceed with converting your van into your dream home.

Chapter 1: Considerations for Choosing the Right Vehicle

If you look at any Van Life-themed social media account, you'll find that the term "van" is somewhat open to interpretation. You'll see a fair share of classic vans, such as Volkswagen Vanagons, Westphalia, and Transporters. You'll also see conversion vans, cargo vans, and European camper vans. But the lifestyle also extends to "skoolies," or converted school buses. This, in turn, has inspired folks to convert buses of all kinds. Inventive folks have also taken to converting campers from part-time vacation homes to full time homes on wheels.

So, when you start searching for your new home, you might be completely stalled at how many options are available. In a nutshell, your decision will be driven by a lot of personal factors. Let's examine these further.

Determining Vehicle Size

There's a considerable amount of difference in size between a skoolie and a VW Transporter, just as there's a huge difference between a three-bedroom house and a studio apartment.

One of the first things you'll need to consider is how much space you need. There are a lot of elements that can go into this part of your accommodations.

1. The number of passengers — and their species!
2. The length of the trip
3. The amenities, such as a bathroom, food preparation area, etc
4. Personal preference

The number of passengers will, of course, dictate how many seats and how many sleeping areas you will need in your van. If you'll have children with you, you might feel most comfortable if they're able to be safely belted into fixed seats while the vehicle is moving. While nearly every veteran van lifer has an amusing story of using a cooler as a seat, it's frowned upon by the law and definitely not safe!

If you're bringing your Adventure Pup or a Feline Mascot (neither of which is unheard of!), you'll have to plan to accommodate their needs, as well. For dogs, you'll want to make sure you have room for them to rest while you drive, move around as they wish when they're not on an adventure with you, and a spot for them to sleep. This can mean making room for a dog bed or making room in your bed for a dog. Cats typically need around 16-18 square feet of space to feel comfortable. They'll also need a litter pan that won't slosh all over the floor of the van unless otherwise toilet trained. Many people do share their van life with a furry friend, so it can be done, with careful planning!

The second part of determining space from the number of passengers is based on comfort level. If you are currently sharing a three-bedroom house with two children and a dog, You're accustomed to a certain amount of space in which to maneuver. Even in the largest bus, you will still run into each other, and you will find privacy a very rare element, indeed. However, if you're currently sharing a studio with your partner, then you're already well-prepared for the challenges that come with cohabitating in a tiny space.

The length of the trip will also dictate the size of vehicle you need, if largely from the standpoint of accommodating four seasons worth of equipment and clothing. If you plan on making your van your permanent home, then you'll need to consider how you'll plan for the seasonal changes. Perhaps you take the opportunity to "chase the weather" and always park somewhere where the weather is dry and warm. Perhaps you choose a vehicle with additional storage for rain gear, snow gear, heavier blankets or sleeping bags, and fans for hot weather.

If you have the opportunity to stop and regroup periodically through your trip, you won't need to stash as much stuff. If you have a small storage unit (or a friend or relative who's willing to let you borrow some space), you can swing by as the situation calls for to change out your equipment, clothing, and more. Granted, this means you'll have to plan ahead to drive to that specific location in time, but it can save you hundreds of pounds and several square feet of extra "stuff" you don't need to carry with you everywhere.

The next consideration is how you will use the room within your vehicle. If you plan to have a bathroom area, you're likely going to want a camper- or bus-type set up. If you instead plan to pack a portable toilet and bucket-style shower, you can really make any type of vehicle work. We'll discuss this in more detail shortly, but at this stage, you'll want to consider if you want to have a full water closet with plumbing or if you can deal with an alternative plan.

The same is true for food preparation areas. The most rugged vans might have a cooler and a propane burner. The most luxurious have full oven ranges, small refrigerators, kitchen sinks, and cabinets. In between are an almost infinite variety of choices. We'll discuss kitchen needs and practical applications in a later section too, but at this stage, consider how much room you feel will be necessary for the kind of food prep you plan. If you're going to install plumbing, gas, or electricity for this, it's best to think of it now.

Lastly, your own personal preferences are something you truly need to consider. On paper, a solo voyager needs only a driver's seat and a bed, with room for storage. In reality, you might find yourself feeling very claustrophobic. The opposite can be true, too. You might find yourself overwhelmed by the size of your space and the maintenance required to keep it clean and functional.

One practical test that is recommended by all sorts of van life experts is the "try it at home" test. Before purchasing a van, bus, or camper of any kind, look up the approximate dimensions of space within the vehicle. Next, find a space in your home, garage, yard, basement, etc., and tape off those exact dimensions. Some experts recommend hanging sheets or shower curtains to give the illusion of the van walls, but you may be able to get a feel for what you'll be working with without going that far.

Without anything in it, how does this space feel? Now start adding objects to the area, either figuratively by marking off the space with tape or chalk, or literally. How big is the sleeping area? If you take that portion away, how well can you maneuver in the remaining space? There will be a learning curve when you actually start living in a van, but if you feel uncomfortable with the space before it's even "real," then you'll definitely want to consider a different option.

Another thing to keep in mind is the height of the van. If you're going with a regular-style van that does not have a pop-top, you may not be able to stand fully upright in the back. For those who are planning to use the van only as a place to sleep and store things, this might be perfectly acceptable. For others, this might be extremely limiting. Again, this comes down to personal preference, but it is definitely something you'll want to consider before you invest in your new home on wheels.

Vehicle Specifications

Beyond the considerations of space, there is the fact that you will have to drive this vehicle from time to time!

Of course, size is a consideration when operating a vehicle, as well. You should feel comfortable driving your van, camper, or bus in a variety of conditions, including on regular city streets, on the highway, on unmaintained or unpaved roads, and also be able to park and reverse.

While your particular trip might not include all of these elements, there will be times when something unforeseen occurs, and you'll need to make do. For example, there are parts of the country where the detour for a temporarily closed well-traveled road is a dirt path. Additionally, you might find it necessary to hit the freeway to get to the next closest gas station, even if you've carefully planned to avoid cities as much as possible. Therefore, it's important to be able to safely guide your vehicle wherever you happen to roam.

If you plan to frequently encounter those unmaintained and unpaved roads, you'll also want to pay close attention to your drivetrain. A drivetrain contains the parts (components) of a vehicle that deliver power to certain wheels.

Let's look at the differences:

- Two-wheel drive (2WD). If your van is referred to as "rear-wheel drive" or "front-wheel drive," it's a 2WD model.
    - Rear-wheel drive delivers the power to the back wheels, and thus the vehicle is "pushed" forward from behind, so the front wheels can handle steering. Many sports cars are RWD, resulting in a balanced, powerful drive. On the flip side, RWD vehicles perform poorly in wet or freezing conditions.
    - Front-wheel drive delivers power to the front wheels, where the engine weight provides balance that improves overall traction. These vehicles typically have a more respectable fuel economy, as well, which can be important to your budget.

- Four-wheel drive (4WD). This option allows drivers to select between RWD and 4WD, depending on the terrain. 4WD delivers power to all four wheels simultaneously, which is fantastic when taking on tough terrain but terrible for your fuel economy. This is why engineers offer the ability to turn off 4WD when the conditions don't require it.
- All-wheel drive (AWD). This option is becoming more and more popular with larger vehicles. AWD requires a front, rear, and central differential, which means all four wheels have power when they need it. A lot of modern (post-2015) heavy-duty vehicles offer this type of drivetrain as an option. Automatic AWD operates in 2WD until the computer sensors determine extra power is needed in a specific location. It is unlikely that you will find this feature on a bus or older van, however.

The rest of the vehicle options you'll need to choose between are far more intuitive. Do you want an engine that runs on regular gasoline or diesel? Check the specifications for any vehicle you're interested in to determine what kind of fuel it needs, as well as the overall fuel economy.

What about transmission? Can you drive a standard, or will an automatic transmission be the best option for you and any others who will be along for the trip? While fans of each option can debate the merits and downfalls of each for eternity, the reality, in this case, is that you'll need to be able to choose a van you can regularly drive without issue.

Insurance

We won't go into too much detail on this topic because requirements and options vary from state to state and country to country. Still, insurance is a very important part of the equation. Not only will you need to have insurance on your vehicle if you plan to drive anywhere, but you'll want to make sure your contents are covered, as well.

Before you purchase any van, bus, or camper, speak with your insurance representative. You'll want to make sure you're covered not only as a driver but also for any accidents that might befall your new home. There are plenty of situations that might render your vehicle undrivable or your quarters unliveable. You need to make sure you're protected not just on the road but for your lifestyle, as well.

When you speak to your insurance representative, make sure you bring up all of these concerns and receive a quote. You will need to decide if you prefer to budget for a higher level of insurance coverage or put away enough savings as a cushion for any mishaps that occur. While it may seem early to think about this, it's crucial that you are able to afford the insurance on any vehicle you might take out on the road. Otherwise, it's simply not the vehicle for you!

Chapter 2: So Many Choices!

If you were to type the word "van" into Google, you'd probably get far, far more information than you could rationally digest in one sitting. Therefore, we'll quickly run through the different types of vehicles you might consider, as well as some factors that might go into your decision to purchase — or stay far away from — that type.

There are plenty of nuances and adaptations to each and every individual van, so it would be impossible to review every single brand that has ever been used for van life. Instead, we'll look at the overall classes of van, and remember — these are just basic guidelines. As they say on the road, "Your Mileage May Vary!"

Classic Vans

These are your Vanagons, your Westphalia, Transporters, and all of the Instagram-ready VW campers that fit the expected stereotype. This class can also include any pre-1990 vans from any manufacturer.

Speaking from an aesthetic point of view, these vehicles are often very photogenic and will get tons of attention on the road. They've got that "old school" appeal that dredges up pleasant, nostalgic memories in nearly anyone who traveled extensively in childhood.

There is, in fact, a huge community of Classic Van Lifers, so you'll be able to connect with plenty of folks who have extensively driven, maintained, rehabbed, worked on, lived in, or are in any possible way familiar with these vans. This is great news for anyone new to van life because you'll have plenty of resources and support through each step of the process.

In fact, when shopping for a Classic Van, you'll find that a large portion of those for sale will be more or less road-ready, due to the fact that many people have purchased and rehabbed these vehicles, then moved on to a bigger and better project following the success of their maiden voyage.

Also, thanks to the recent resurgence in popularity of these vehicles, it's not too difficult to find information that will guide you through basic repairs and maintenance. Since these are vehicles that are actually driven on the road regularly today, it's not too terribly hard to find spare parts, either.

Being able to handle repairs and find spare parts easily is a good thing because you will likely have to do this with frequency, unfortunately. Older vehicles, no matter how well maintained, are prone to breakdowns. Hoses wear out, parts get bent, you might run too hot or too cold, and things will simply stop working over time. If you choose an older vehicle like a Classic Van, try to get as complete a service history as possible. You might also luck out and find one with a new or refurbished engine, but always inspect all of the mechanical aspects — you never know when one of them is going to show their age.

Another consideration is the maintenance you can't handle on your own. Some of the older, foreign-built vehicles require special tools, parts, or mechanical knowledge. Rather than being able to breeze into any auto mechanic's garage, you will need to make sure someone on staff can repair your year, make, and model of the van. A breakdown is always inconvenient, but extra frustrating when you have to spend time and energy figuring out where to go for assistance.

Additionally, things like "fuel efficiency" and "safety technology" are relatively new terms in the automotive world. Unlike today's vehicles, the vans of the 1960s didn't need to meet speed limits of 70 miles per hour regularly. Seatbelts didn't become mandatory until 1968. Airbags didn't become a requirement until 1998. Though Classic Vans are built like actual tanks in many regards, they are — by and large — lacking in the modern technology of current vehicles.

Conversion Vans

A Conversion Van is a type of van that is able to "convert" to a livable space. Early conversion vans of the 1970s simply added extra seating, or seats that folded into beds, and plush features, like carpeting and interior lighting. In the 1980s and 90s, features like televisions, VCRs, and indoor-style outlets were added to the category. Conversion vans are insulated, ventilated, and may be equipped with an isolated battery for a non-engine power source. In many ways, conversion vans are not unlike some of today's standard SUVs. But, even the most well-equipped conversion van will require some adaptation in order to be a full-time home.

Conversion vans are typically not too terribly expensive to purchase or maintain. It's relatively easy to find an older Chevy, Ford, or Dodge conversion van that has decent bones at a decent price. Since these vans are usually based on, very similar to, or completely identical to regular passenger vans, it's easy to find parts, and you won't need to find a mechanic who specializes in your particular van.

Spending less on the vehicle itself means you can allocate more funds toward the customization of the vehicle. It's also very likely that you'll find a Conversion Van that has some of the parts and pieces that you'll want in your finished van. For example, a lot of Conversion Vans have outward-swinging doors instead of sliding doors. Many manufacturers use this option as a way to stash fold-out tables or storage, which you can incorporate into your overall van scheme. Many also have built-in storage, which you can expand upon or leave as-is. You'll be able to enjoy seats with seatbelts that then fold into beds, saving you the problem of seats and beds as separate entities.

Some Conversion Vans were created with higher roofs, which may allow you to stand up comfortably but will definitely let you take advantage of more storage opportunities along the walls or roof.

Cargo Vans

Cargo Vans share the same advantages as Conversion Vans when it comes to being regularly maintained. Cargo Vans are being manufactured to this day, often as part of vehicle fleets for commercial and industrial businesses. Typically, Cargo Vans have a completely empty body, aside from a driver and passenger seat. Some have old tool racks, storage cabinets, or hanging storage in the back, depending on what they were used for in their past life. You may choose to incorporate or remove these to start fresh.

One thing that many Van Lifers enjoy about Cargo Vans is that they have very few windows. That means any wall is appropriate for building or storing. That also means you don't have to worry about looky-loos peeping in your van when it's parked or while you're sleeping.

On the flip side, both cargo and conversion vans typically have a lower fuel economy. While most options will function on regular unleaded gasoline, which tends to be less expensive, you will be stopping at fuel stations more regularly. You may also wish to keep spare fuel on hand for emergency situations.

You might find that many of the cargo vans on the market have very high mileage, especially if they were regularly used as part of a business. The advantage to this is that business vehicles are usually well-maintained since they're a crucial part of the operation. Still, you'll want to be prepared for any aging vehicle maintenance requirements that might come up.

Depending on your willingness to invest time and money into the van project, having no basic setup in a cargo van might also be a disadvantage.

After all, you will need to create a liveable space out of nothing. You can find rehabbed cargo vans for sale, but these will cost more than a completely blank slate, of course. We'll talk more about what it takes to rehab and fully construct a living space in a van in the next chapter, but this is definitely something to keep in mind at this stage of the game, as well.

Euro Vans

First, bear in mind that the term "Euro Van" can refer to two different things. First, a Volkswagen Eurovan is a very specific make and model of van. These pop-top vans were offered in the US between 1993 and 2003, and many are still around and functional today.

There are others who refer to any European touring-style van as a "Euro Van." This can include Mercedes Sprinters, Klassen vans, Fiat Ducato, Renault Trafic, and other vehicles manufactured overseas. With the exception of the Mercedes Sprinter, it's not often you'll find these types of vans in the United States; however, with the growing market for off-grid options, more and more are arriving stateside.

When you're shopping for anything under the umbrella of "Euro Van," double-check if it's an actual VW Eurovan or a European van conversion.

Interestingly enough, VW Eurovans and Sprinter vans share a lot of common features. For example, they both are designed with large and small cargo storage options. They're more modern vehicles, which means you don't have to dredge up historical data to learn more about how they work. Additionally, as modern vehicles, they're equipped with smaller engines that are more powerful and consume less fuel.

Of course, there's a downside to this: as European creations, you'll need to find a mechanic who understands the engineering. They can also be difficult to find parts for, and expensive to repair. There will be more technical elements, such as computer systems, while the earlier and older models have more manual aspects.

Additionally, one thing to keep in mind about these taller vehicles is that you will need greater clearance. While this is typically not a problem on well-traveled highways, where semis and commuter buses are expected, this may pose a challenge on some of the more off-the-beaten-path locations you wish to visit. You can also encounter issues with parking garages if you find yourself within city limits.

Buses

There is a lot that can be said about buses, but the three basic options are School Bus, Coach, or Transit. Though the term "Skoolie" refers specifically to School Buses, the community as a whole tends to accept nearly any bus under the umbrella term.

There are significant differences between the three. True Skoolies are very affordable. Retired school buses can be acquired from multiple sources, including junkyard auctions, school district dispersal sales, online auctions, and more. There are several different lengths and configurations available as well.

Coach buses are bigger and bulkier than school buses, but they have one significant advantage: Under-cabinet storage. If you've ever traveled the country by bus, you'll recall stowing your bags under the bus at the curb. This is great if you want to take along bicycles or large gear, or need to pack for all seasons. The size of the vehicle can be somewhat daunting though when navigating narrow city streets or winding mountain passages.

Transit buses are retired city buses. Like skoolies, these can come in various shapes and sizes. They rarely have the extra storage, but one unique feature is that some smaller city buses are equipped with wheelchair lifts or entry-assist options, which can be very helpful for those with mobility concerns.

Nearly all buses are equipped with a diesel engine, but some will have the engine in front, while others have the engine in the rear. If you're planning on running plumbing and electric wiring, you'll definitely need to mind the engine. You'll also need to know how to access it for repairs and maintenance, and pack the essential equipment, including any ladders or hydraulic lifts you might need.

One major downside to buses is that repair shops are extremely scarce for these vehicles. They tend to be pretty straightforward in their engineering, so it is possible to learn some DIY repair techniques, but if you're not mechanically inclined, you might have a rough time in the event of a breakdown.

Additionally, insurance can be a bit tricky on buses, but not impossible. As mentioned before, speak to your local representative to get the details before you go on a bus buying spree!

Campers
"Campers" is another somewhat ambiguous term. Some people call any van that you can sleep in a "camper." Others consider pull-behind trailers with living quarters "campers." For some, a "camper" is a full RV. Still others consider a "camper" a trailer that contains nothing more than room to sleep and adequate ventilation and weather protection.

There's a huge difference between an Airstream "camper" and a Patriot "camper" and a Vistabule "camper." When searching and shopping, be fully aware of what anything under the generic term "camper" entails.

For the most part, anything with the title of "camper" will be a prefabricated home on the road. It will include sleep areas, food prep areas, seating areas, and storage. There may be a bathroom, depending on the size of the camper. It may be a trailer instead of a combined living/driving space, such as in a van or a bus. Then again, one man's trailer is another man's camper!

When it comes to choosing the type of vehicle you plan to take on the road, there are really no "wrong" answers. While every class of vehicle has its own community that is completely devoted to that particular model, there are advantages and disadvantages to every single one. You'll find that even within these communities, there will be devotees to a certain year, make, or model.

Therefore, it's really impractical to listen to the recommendations of online forums, friends, or family members unless they face the same exact challenges, situations, and preferences as you will. Instead, pay attention to details. What are the dimensions? How many seats? What kind of engine does it have? What does its maintenance history look like? What type of fuel economy does it get? And most importantly — are you going to feel comfortable living in it?

Chapter 3: Ready-to-Roll, or Ready-to-Rehab?

The next consideration for your van home is how much work you want to put into transforming the space inside into the home of your dreams.

Ask yourself these two questions:

Do you want to create the ultimate space, in which you can comfortably live the rest of your life?

More importantly, are you willing to put in months or even years of hard work in order to create that space?

When asked what was most surprising about the process of gutting and rehabbing a van or bus, nearly everyone who has gone through the exercise will say the time of the entire process. When you browse those gorgeous van homes on the internet, see if you can't research the owners or builders to see how long they spent on the process. Many are very upfront with the process of refurnishing it, including all of the challenges that go along with that. After all, Van Life is a community effort!
Though many of the vans and skoolies you see on social media are labors of love, rebuilt from bare bones, you can start with a fully ready-to-roll vehicle.

Yes, it will cost you more at the outset, but buying a fully rehabbed and refurbed vehicle means you won't have to strip the inside. You won't have to rewire anything. You won't have to learn practical plumbing. You won't have to create structures. You won't have to source lumber, nails, screws, tools, hinges... nothing! You can simply open the doors to your new home, look around, and decide where you want to put your belongings.

If that sounds like an absolute nightmare, then you are clearly more in the "Do It Yourself" camp. Before you purchase a giant transit bus and start demolition, there are a few things you need to ask yourself:

How much time can you devote each day to construction?
For many, construction starts out as a "little bit each day" type of project, but swiftly becomes a full obsession. There will be setbacks. Things will not work out exactly as planned. You will cut a piece of insulation multiple times, trying to get it to fit along a curved wall... and eventually, you will cut it to the point where you can't use it. You will find that the plumbing absolutely cannot go there, or there, or really anywhere that it might make sense. Every person who has ever changed anything about their van has been in this exact position.

And that is how we become obsessed — this drive to solve all problems immediately takes over all reason. At the same time, you might still be working your day job as you work on your van space. Your partner, your children, your dog and cat, might all be rightfully concerned that you're spending all night in the van.

This is an easy way to burn yourself out on the whole project. As you encounter one frustration after another, you might decide it's not worth it. While we have no practical cures for the difficulties you'll no doubt encounter, it is highly recommended that you work on your van or bus slowly and surely, rather than trying to rush through it. If you're planning a very extensive makeover, don't plan to leave in two months.
A simple rule of thumb: If time is of the essence, choose something that's ready to go (or at least very close). If you want to really create something

from the ground up, don't have a deadline.

Can You Build It?

Be very honest with yourself: do you know anything about construction, electricity, plumbing, insulation, drywall, cabinetry, etc.? Or, are you handy enough that you feel very confident about learning? Can you see a straight line, take a variety of accurate measurements, and execute the product in your mind?

There are four main steps to the process of creating your dream space inside a van.

First, you need to gut it. This is especially true if you purchase a bus that still has the seats inside. You will need to remove everything, and you will need to somehow get rid of it or repurpose it.

As a side note, you will need to be creative when it comes to the collection of school bus seats you're about to have if you've gone with a skoolie. Some folks have luck selling them "as is" to people in the area or via online auctions. More likely, you'll want to take them apart and sell the metal for scrap. Unless you have loads of space in which to store dozens of seats, this is something you ought to plan on doing before you bring your skoolie home, too.

Once you've got your open space, you need a functional design. You'll need to consider not just the overall flow, but where you're going to put the heaviest weight loads, where you're going to put storage or built-ins, and the reality of where you can put plumbing or electricity, which might be based on where you put the water source or hook up, generator, or solar panels. You'll need to be aware of where and how the doors open, as well as the windows.

Most people who have completely gutted and refurbished a van report having at least two to three versions of their design plans, so don't be too concerned if your first plan has to be scrapped. Learn, and move on.

Next comes executing the design. You'll need to run any electric and plumbing before you put in insulation and walls. You'll have to put in walls before you build structures, such as cabinets, seating areas, or sleeping areas.

A side note about storage: One of the best ways to maximize storage is to put it under seating or sleeping areas. One very popular trick is to raise the sleeping area as high as you can, to create a larger storage space beneath. You can build the frame of your bed over a cabinet system to create both open and closed storage underneath your bed. Perhaps you add a fold-out table to the base of your bed or seating that pulls out like a drawer. The options are infinite!

As you are constructing your new home, you will need both materials and tools. Of the two, the tools might be the most cost-prohibitive, as well as the hardest to source. You will also make multiple trips to the hardware store each week. Therefore, you must account in your budget for tools, supplies, as well as gas money and time spent at the hardware store acquiring these things. You might see if there is a tool-lending program in your community, as this can save you several hundred dollars. You might also cruise local selling walls to see if there are used tools available in your area. The unfortunate truth about these processes though, is that you might not find what you need exactly when you need it.

Despite all of your best intentions, there will be waste. Anything from bent nails to stripped screws, to perfectly usable lumber cut to the wrong length. You will not want to keep this waste forever, so consider a plan that will allow you to collect, remove, and appropriately dispose of it. This may mean a call to a junkyard or working with your regular waste management company.

Can You Afford It?

The cost figures for fully renovating a skoolie range from $10,000 to $30,000. Granted, that's cost over time, and as mentioned earlier, it can take years to fully construct the space of your dreams.

We've alluded to some of the expenses here, but let's put it all on the table.

You'll need:

- tools
- safety equipment, such as goggles and gloves
- lumber
- screws, nails, hinges, knobs, sliding rails, bolts, and anchors
- wiring
- insulation
- plugs and switches
- pipes
- walls
- countertops/ sealed surfaces
- flooring
- faucets and fixtures for water closet

This doesn't include any decorative items, such as backsplashes or paint, or power and water supplies, which we'll discuss in more detail in the next chapter. It also doesn't include any books, courses, or instruction you might pay for to help you with your endeavors.

Do You Have the Work Space?

If you're going to be working on a vehicle for months or years, you need a space where you can safely and legally do so.

It is unlikely that a skoolie will fit in the garage of your suburban home. It is also unlikely that you'll be permitted to work extensively on demo and rehab in the parking garage of a city condo building. If you know someone who has a large yard where you can work, that might be a great option... until the neighbors call the city.

There are legal considerations for working on vehicles within some city or corporation limits. Even if you're not disposing of harmful liquids, less enthusiastic neighbors might consider your activities a nuisance. Therefore, you'll want to find a nice, large space — preferably indoors — where you can work on your vehicle. And then a backup location. And possibly even a backup to the backup. Whether you wear out your welcome or simply outgrow your space, you'll need a plan, since you can't just plop a large bus or very tall van down anywhere.

Most beginner van projects are somewhere in between "completely ready" and "completely reconstructed." You might choose a "mostly ready" van, and lift the bed to add storage or shorten the sleeping area to add a food prep area. You might start with only the minimal changes, then add a little room here or include a fold-out table there as you spend time living in your new space.

Alternatively, you might feel that life on the road is not complete unless you have a wood-burning stove, fully functional skylights, and a hand-painted porcelain backsplash in the bathroom. There's nothing wrong with this perspective, either.

Ultimately, creating your van space is a balance between what you *want* to do, and what you *can* do. If there is a significant overlap between the two, then best wishes on your rehab and refurb experience! If you find that you're lacking in time, skill, funds, or space, you might scale back your project. You might wish to find a mostly-ready van or add the assistance of a professional if the issue is time or skill.

The internet is full of experiences shared by those who have made this journey before. We'll share a few links in the **resources guide** to get you started. When it comes to the building stage, however, you truly cannot research too much, especially if you are a novice DIY-er. You'll want to consider safety, practicality, usability, and durability of everything you construct to be 100% sure before you lay the first nail or cut the first board!

And most of all, have patience and faith. Whether or not it turns out exactly as you dreamed, it will turn out exactly as you have built it. Your planning and patience will pay off in the end.

Chapter 4: Budget Considerations for Creating Your Van

While it may seem that we harp and harp on the concept of budget, you'll find that this is with good reason. One of the most common reasons people give up on the van life dream is because they run out of money before they even have the chance to hit the road.

While it's true that you can save quite a bit of money by abandoning regular bills, multiple car payments, mortgages, and the like with the vagabond lifestyle of the road, you will need to invest a bit of money into setting up the lifestyle to be sustainable.

For those who feel cooped up, you might be so passionately drawn to the experience that you feel like you could simply hop in any old van and drive off and "make it work." There is a very specific demographic for whom this is true. If you have plenty of money, the ability to take on any odd jobs no matter where you are, no particular preference about where you sleep at night, a decent cooler, and a reliable propane burner, then it is possible to "make it work."

If you have a family, pets, the desire to have a predictable shower and bathroom experience, the ability to prepare a variety of fresh foods, and the need to sleep in a comfortable bed, then you will need to plan very carefully in the early stages.

So, when it comes to budgeting, we started at the overall "big picture" of all of the various categories of expenses that might come into play. Now it's time to start drilling down into more detail, starting with the van itself.

How Much Will It Cost to Hit the Road?

The equation for determining the overall cost of your van is as follows:

Cost of Vehicle + Cost of Repairs/Rehab/Refurb = Pre-Road Cost

(Cost of oil/oil change x 6) + cost of tires + cost for replacement cost + hourly rate for emergency maintenance = Annual Upkeep Cost

Size of fuel tank x Average Miles Per Gallon = Miles Per Tank
Total Distance Traveled (divided by) Miles Per Tank = Total Number of Fuel Stops
(Size of fuel tank x going rate for fuel) x Number of Fuel Stops = Total Fuel Budget

Pre-Road Cost + Annual Upkeep Cost + Total Fuel Budget is the amount you will need to get you through the first year on the road.

There are ways to maximize your money, however.

First, remember that the bigger the vehicle, the more fuel it will need. Consider purchasing the smallest possible van or bus that you can actually live in. This might require you to do the "try it at home" test a few times with different configurations.

In addition, consider planning your wandering strategically. Instead of California one week and Connecticut the next, consider taking some time to wind along the West Coast. Try finding a good central location where you can park for a longer period of time, and use a bicycle or small motorbike or scooter to explore the sights nearby. This will not only save fuel costs but wear and tear costs on your van as a whole, minimizing maintenance costs. Lastly, if you find a free spot to camp within National Lands, you'll save a significant amount of money on camp fees and site fees while you do this exploration. Another thing to keep in mind when looking at the annual budget is your income. We'll discuss working from the road in more detail shortly, but there are ways to make money while you travel. Any income you make will offset your expenses, of course, and can either go toward regular maintenance and fuel or toward an emergency fund.

Power and Water: The Utilities

There are also some features you can add to the van construction that will help you save, as well. If you add a power supply and water supply, you'll have a fully self-sustaining home on wheels. This means you'll have a lower reliance on stopping at full-service camping parks. You'll be able to produce the power to charge your phones and devices, as well as have a functioning bathroom to help with showers and general clean up.

When it comes to power supplies, the top two options are generators and solar power. Each option has, of course, strong arguments for and against them.

First, let's look at generators:

Pros	Cons
Produce a lot of instant power at any time	Noisy
Not weather dependent	Require fuel and ongoing maintenance
Can handle a lot of wattage	May be prohibited in some locations due to fumes

Now let's look at the argument surrounding solar power:

Pros	Cons
No fumes, no noise, no maintenance	Does not create a lot of power
Can be repositioned as necessary	Power supply is dependent upon intake/positioning
No on-going expenses: install and done	Can be damaged, which requires replacement

All said, it boils down to your personal preference and budget. A generator will be an ongoing expense but will be able to supply great quantities of instant power. This might be a greater advantage than disadvantage if you're going to need to power a laptop, phone, and WiFi hotspot. On the other hand, if you won't need tons of power all the time, solar panels might be a real budget-saving option.

There are Van Lifers who live without power. You can choose this route as well. Between independent battery charge units, USB plugs in more modern vehicles, and the old-fashioned type of plug that uses a decommissioned cigarette lighter port, it's possible to keep a cell phone charged. You can also take breaks at fast food restaurants, rest stations, or laundromats, and mooch a little power while you fuel your own body, shower, or catch up on some laundry. Before you help yourself to some power, make sure it's allowed. It also probably goes without saying, but never leave your phone unattended, as it will very likely take a voyage of its own. And if you're going to borrow a little electricity, it's considered good road manners if you make a purchase while you're there.

The next consideration is the water supply. If you are going to carry your own water supply, you'll need two tanks — one for freshwater, and one for greywater. Most experts recommend each tank hold up to 5-7 gallons. The main factor in deciding how big of a tank you want is how much you can carry yourself, as you'll be responsible for filling, maintaining, and emptying these tanks. One gallon of water weighs approximately 8 pounds, for reference. Therefore, a five-gallon tank will be a heft of close to 50 pounds, once you include the weight of the tank itself.

You'll also want to make sure that any tank, pipes, or tubing involved with your freshwater supply is FDA-rated as food safe.

Greywater tanks do not have to be food-safe, but are just as important. "Greywater" refers to wastewater from your sink, shower, etc.

You'll want to make sure that both your freshwater and greywater tanks are both accessible and secured, so they are equally available for filling and emptying, and don't slosh around while you drive.

If you're looking for a very simple way to access freshwater, consider the gravity method. This basically involves installing the water supply in a way that gravity delivers the water through the tubing, to your waiting hands, cup, bucket, or wherever you need the water to go. Many rudimentary van shower systems use this method by hanging the water supply over a door or from an overhead hook, and releasing a valve so the water flows freely.

For those who wish to have more control over water flow, a manual hand or foot pump can be installed. Hand pumps require very little mechanical know-how and involve a temporary or fixed pump being added to the open end of the freshwater tank. The design is not unlike a soap or lotion bottle pump dispenser, only on a larger scale. Foot pumps will require a directed flow via a faucet and sink so that the greywater tank catches the runoff and waste, but they offer excellent control over how much water is dispensed at a time.

Lastly, there's the option of an electric water pump. For this option, you will likely prefer a generator that you can run at least part-time to assist with the process, as you'll need at least 12 volts of electricity. With this choice, you do have the option to install a water heater so that you'll have continuous hot water, as well. You can also add an accumulator, which will store a little water each time the water is turned on. The accumulator will let you use a bit of water even when the power is off, which will save on noise and expense.

Then there's the toilet. Technology has come a long way in this regard, so your van won't have to be as primitive as you fear... unless, of course, you want it that way. There are a variety of road-ready commodes available that can be incorporated into your new abode with or without plumbing.

First, there are composting toilets. These toilets are chemical-free and store your waste until you can dispose of it. The secret is a peat mixture and a dehydration process. The liquids go into a separate bottle, which can be dumped securely, while the solids mix with the peat and turn into safe compost. These toilets do require power in order to work, however, as most include a small fan that keeps the process working. Composting toilets can be very expensive, but a very wise investment for those who wish to use the toilet indoors with the most minimal need for chemicals, hassle, or interacting with the resulting matter.

Then there are portable potties. These are small, self-contained toilet units that can be installed anywhere. They feature a waste tank and a water tank and can be "flushed" like a standard toilet, although what's flushed will await future disposal in the appropriate tank. This means that chemicals should be used to keep odor at bay between emptyings, though eco-friendly chemicals are also readily available. These toilets do use a considerable amount of water and can get heavy depending on how long you go between emptying.

Those traveling with children or in groups may want to invest in a full electric camper-style toilet. While impractical to install on a smaller van, this format is suitable for buses, where a waste tank can be stashed under the vehicle and dumped appropriately in waste stations at campgrounds. The benefit here is that you don't have an immediate or urgent worry about overflow, no possible spillage, and the toilet is a permanent part of your home. The downside is that it will have to be incorporated and installed, thus taking up valuable space and requiring a sizable investment.

There are also a variety of low-tech options. From what amounts to a stool with no seat, to a bucket with a seat on it, many Van Lifers have made the most of an awkward situation with a practical — if not at all glamorous — solution. There are multiple small battery-operated or hand-pump style toilets on the market as well, but bear in mind, these are often very low to the ground and still require regular and frequent emptying. Also, consider the fact that you may need to use this device at any hour of the day, in all kinds of weather. Make sure you choose a toilet option that you'll feel comfortable with at midnight during a thunderstorm!

It is possible to live without any plumbing whatsoever, of course. Water can be found in many places, and it's very simple to stock up on gallons of usable drinking water. This will, however, require room for storage. A cooler is a multi-level solution when it comes to water usage, as well. The ice used to keep food fresh in a cooler will, over time, melt. While you might not want to use that water for drinking, you can heat it up with your propane burner and a pot, and enjoy a bath or shower. You can also use that melted ice water to cool off when temperatures are climbing. Toilets can be found at gas stations, restaurants, grocery stores, campgrounds, parks, and rest areas.

When disposing of greywater and waste, it is crucial that you do not contaminate any water sources. Make sure you only dump wastewater in approved and appropriate areas. Composting toilets are less dodgy since the waste has been decontaminated naturally, but some toilet solutions include chemicals that can poison humans and wildlife, and destroy native plants and soil. Whenever possible, use biodegradable, environmentally friendly soaps, cleaners, and toilet papers.

If you choose to go the "natural" route, remember to be courteous. Step away from main areas — even if you're camping on free land, you can still avoid areas where people are likely to walk. Dig your waste trench at least six inches deep, and be sure to bury everything thoroughly once you're done.

Chapter 5: The Search Process

Once you've got all of your plans in hand, it's time to make them so. You know what size vehicle you need and likely have a top-three selection of the type of vehicle you'd like to purchase. You are confident about what you want to put in your van or bus, where it's going to go, and what you need to do to make it happen.

Now stack all of those plans neatly, and throw everything on the floor except your budget.

Shopping for your van or bus or camper can be agonizing if you have very specific requirements. You may choose to wait until you are able to locate The Exact Perfect Vehicle for your adventure. Alternatively, you may choose something that is more of a compromise on your exact requests but meets all your requirements. The choice is entirely your own.

The internet is a fantastic place to find Van Life resources. As a community that has no physical footprint (or rather, one that is always in motion), there are many forums and sites where van dwellers meet up to share thoughts, ideas, and ask each other questions. In fact, we've included some of these in the **resource section** of this book.

As you read through these forums, you'll find discussions about particular types of vans or skoolies, as well as sales ads. Some people within the van community make a fair living off rehabbing and selling vehicles. Others find that they "outgrow" their van and are ready to step up to a bigger, more off-road capable, or in some cases, more frugal vehicle.

Another online resource is vehicle sales sites. Again, we've compiled a few suggestions to get you started in the **resource section**. There are sites dedicated to vans and buses, but you can also find some good deals on regular automotive sites, especially if you're looking for a cargo or conversion van that you can take down to the bare floor and remodel into your own.

There is some debate as to whether it's worth it to reach out to regular car dealerships. The answer is yes. Shopping for a van is not unlike shopping for any other specialty item, like antique glass or rare book printings. You never know where they're going to turn up. You might find just the right base vehicle has come into a dealership as a trade-in and swipe it up before they list it on an online auction. One benefit to this plan is that dealers seldom let vehicles leave their lot without at least a full inspection. Though they might not take the time, or invest the money into fixing anything that's out of sorts, they'll at least be aware and disclose this information to you.

Auctions are another great resource, if you're ok with buying vehicles "as is." You might not know its issues, problems, or need for repairs until you get it home and start truly inspecting it, but the vehicle you purchase at an auction can be extremely cheap.

Online auctions have similar perils — you are relying on the word of the person selling the vehicle, and you may not be able to physically inspect the vehicle until you have already paid for it. Still, online auction sites can bring great luck to those who have done their homework and are ready for just about anything.

If you're specifically looking for a bus, you can reach out directly to the source for more information about obtaining one of their decommissioned vehicles. For skoolies, you can reach out to the school district. Frequently, their vehicles pass through local auto auctions, but it's possible the school district might be interested in making a deal, for the right price.

When it comes to coach-type buses, you might need to do a bit more digging. National bus lines will have a point of contact for decommissioned buses, but if you're dealing with a more local outfit, it might require a few calls and emails before you find the right person.

The city transit department will likely have information about what happens to city buses once they're removed from duty. In many cases, they end up in junkyards, auctions, or are donated to various programs, but again, you might be able to make arrangements for purchase first.

When it comes to pulling the trigger and purchasing your vehicle, you must feel fully confident in your decision. You must have addressed all budget considerations, all repair requirements, and be ready to shoulder the burden of any rehab and remodeling that will be needed to make your van or bus your new home.

We encourage everyone to do as much research as possible. Find a handful of options. Decide what things you can compromise on and what features are absolute necessities. Can you wiggle on price? What if you find a vehicle that has higher mileage than you'd like, but the price is perfect, and it's been well-cared for? It is highly unlikely that you'll find a vehicle that meets all of your needs precisely. What is far more likely is that you'll find a vehicle that shows you what features, options, and qualities are really most important to you.

If it is at all possible, try to test drive the vehicle. This might mean doing some traveling. Worse yet — this might mean getting your hopes up, traveling, and discovering it's not going to work.

You will have to feel comfortable driving your new home. In the case of a larger bus, it will take time before driving such a massive vehicle feels natural, but if a simple trip around the block feels desperately uncomfortable for any reason, it might be a good time to head back to the drawing board. There are things that can be altered, improved, or modified, but if you decide you really don't like the way driving a van with a manual transmission feels, it might be less expensive to check out options with an automatic transmission, rather than replace the entire system.

You'll also want the opportunity to really inspect the vehicle in detail. This means you might have to take a crash course in the year, make, and model of the vehicle you're going to check out, but it's better to be fully informed than guessing.

Additionally, see what maintenance and repair records you can get your hands on. The more you know about this particular vehicle's history, the more you can plan for future issues — or at least identify what needs your immediate attention.

Advice from the Road- Part 2

When it came to purchasing our first van, I was adamant that it would have a kitchenette, or at least a purposed food-prep area with storage and running water. My plans for the interior included a fold-out table, which I could use as a work station during the day, and could do extra duty as an eating surface, a drying rack for dishes and laundry, or a spot where we could hang out and play games or plan the next leg of our voyage.

I wanted an automatic transmission. I wanted a vehicle no more than 25 years old. I was fine with higher mileage, as long as it was well-cared for and didn't come with any major problems. I didn't care about color, and I wasn't fussy about how the sleeping area was set up.

We ended up with a VW Vanagon from the 1980s. It did not have a kitchen area. It didn't have a fold-out table. It didn't have so much as a shelf. In the back was a platform and a mattress... that's it.

Instead, it had a recently replaced engine. It has been regularly serviced for the past 30 years. It had only two owners and still had its original owner's manual (which is roughly the same size as a 1980s phone book, by the way). It came with a automatic transmission, as he hoped, and a gaudy peace sign sticker... which actually hid a deep ding in the side of the door.

Was it the van I had planned on purchasing? Absolutely not. Was I completely wooed by its mechanical soundness, ease of operation, and blank-slate space? Very much so.

We looked at several dozen vans. Some of them we just courted online until the inevitable Huge Issue came to light. We had the chance to kick some of the tires. But when we found this van, two states away, in a heated, climate-controlled garage, I knew that this was the main contender for our future home on wheels.

Section 3: Creating and Maintaining a Budget While on the Road

There are so many factors that go into both creating and maintaining a budget while you're on the road. Here we'll attempt to walk through the process in easy-to-handle pieces.

If you've even started considering your Van Life budget, your head is probably a whirlwind of figures, with questions like:

1. What can I afford to spend each month?
2. What splurges or luxury items will I allow myself?
3. What happens if I run out of money?
4. If I buy this item now, will it cost me more or less in the long run?
5. What'll I do in an emergency? (Followed by feelings of desperation and panic, usually.)

First, take a deep breath. Having an emergency while on the road is really no different than having an emergency at any other time of your life. You can't completely prepare for everything, and while it's going to be deeply inconvenient, you'll have to take everything step by step to move in the right direction.

As for the rest of the questions, we'll address them one by one. While we can't actually sit down with you and do the math for your particular situation, we can bring you some key points and advice from folks who have been on the road, to help you decide where to spend money, where to save money, and where to make money.

Advice from the Road: Part 3

When we first took our van out, we had nothing. Ok, that's not entirely true. We had a bed, tons of really intuitive storage, a large ice-vault type cooler with a valve on the side to empty out the water, and a propane burner with two fuel tanks. Our van didn't even have interior lights until we removed the non-functioning air conditioning unit and accidentally reconnected something.

We thought this was the best way to save money — live as basically and frugally as possible, right? Barebones means no waste, little investment, and a smaller budget. Well, it turns out that we accidentally sabotaged ourselves with this mindset.

We stocked up on what we considered "van food" beforehand. As experienced campers and hikers, we assumed we'd want to eat the same sort of thing in the van that we ate while camping. We thought we were brilliant.

Well, it turns out that, when you're parked in a camp park full of families grilling huge, juicy steaks, that dehydrated chicken curry packet doesn't look so appetizing anymore. Even worse, because your home has wheels, and because you can get an internet signal nearly anywhere, it is very, very tempting to find yourself at the local famous restaurant every night. Which would you prefer: a powdered camping meal or authentic mole enchiladas served by a woman who has her family's 300-year-old recipe?

It's easy to make excuses, too. After all, you're on the road to experience the world as it is, and that includes the local flavor — literally. Problem is, eating at restaurants eats your budget right up!

So, you learn to compromise. Head to local markets and grocery stores, and stock up on local products there. We could buy all the flavors we couldn't find at home and take them with us wherever we went.

We did have to change the cooler setup, though. We thought we were being budget-conscious by getting the less expensive cooler. Unfortunately, we ended up wasting a lot of food when it got "drowned" in the melting ice.

As a result, we had to modify our entire setup. Just for food? No — to make the most out of our budget. Our no-power, no-water setup was tweaked into a solution that actually reduced our spending. We use only three 160-watt solar panels, which connect to four batteries. These also keep us working while we're on the road. We no longer have to stop at cafes or restaurants and buy something for the privilege of "borrowing" *electricity and WiFi — we're self-reliant. (Think about it — even if you just buy a $3 snack each day for an hour of guilt-free power, that's $90 a month, and that's with a very low estimate!)*

Even better, we have far less food waste. We invested in a more expensive cooler, which plugs into the van's cigarette lighter socket while we're on the road and can connect with the solar battery converter when we're not in motion. Just in case, we have several cooler packs that don't leak, spill, or otherwise ruin our food. We also have a full series of BPA-free food storage containers of all sizes, so if we do need to temporarily run on ice, we lose nothing.

Do we still try out local cuisine at restaurants? Sure, from time to time. But choosing to be able to store and prepare our own fresh food is a decision that required a little more spending on the front end but has saved us literally thousands of dollars each month!

Chapter 1: Determining Your Budget

At its core, a budget is simply a balance between money you have and money you need (or want) to spend. When you live in a fixed, permanent location, it's pretty easy to see what you have, what you need, and what to expect from month to month. After all, our daily routines rarely change overall — and that's why the road is calling to you!

Still, there's something to be said for predictability. Most of us rest easier with at least some perceived control over our daily, weekly, and monthly expenses.

It may feel, at first, like heading out on the road is going to be a complete upheaval of your way of life. In many ways, this is true. But there are plenty of things that aren't going to change about your lifestyle. You'll still need to eat every day. You'll still need to drink plenty of water. You'll still have dirty laundry.

We've included a chart that includes some common ongoing expenses. Bear in mind that this chart only includes expenses that you'll encounter on a continuous basis—we'll get to the start up and packing expenses in a moment.

This is, of course, just a guide to get you started. If you have children on the trip, some of these categories might change a bit. The maintenance for any equipment you install, such as toilets, generators, hot water heaters, and such, will be dependent on what type of equipment you choose and its specific requirements. If you have a pet, you'll need to take their needs into consideration. However, this chart should get you started in the process of thinking about what you need on a running basis.

Expense Category	Considerations	Your Calculation
Fuel	Price per Gallon Miles per Gallon Distance Traveled Fuel Cost Fluctuations (by location) Emergency Fuel Supply	
Maintenance	Oil changes (5-10,000 miles) Tire rotation (5-7,000 miles) Air filter Fluids (Radiator, Transmission, Coolant, Brake, Air Conditioning, Washer, Power Steering) Glass Cracks Windshield Wiper Blades	
Location	Parking pass Camping pass Park entry fees Showers Hotels (if necessary) Greywater dump fees (charged at some campsites)	
Kitchen Supplies	Drinking water Food/Groceries x number of travellers and pets Cleaning tools	

Health	Toiletries (shampoo, toothpaste, soap, etc.) Vitamins Medications (both prescription and OTC) First Aid supplies (bandages, antiseptic cream, cotton swabs) Sunscreen Bug spray Regular medical check-ups, vaccines, dental care
Laundry	Detergent Laundromat costs
Entertainment	Entry fees Park passes Restaurants Cafes/Wineries/Breweries/Distilleries/etc. Gifts/games/toys
Other ongoing expenses	Insurance (Medical, Vehicle, etc.) Generator upkeep (if used) Vet bills (if you bring a pet) Credit card bills Van payment (if you take out a loan for the van) Roadside Assistance Program Cell phone bill WiFi
Expenses from Home (applies only if you choose to maintain your home while you're on the road)	Mortgage/rent Electric/gas/water House sitter/tenant Insurance Taxes

When you're filling out these expenses, try to be both practical and generous in your estimates. No matter where you're traveling, the cost of living is largely based on location. A gallon of water that costs 60 cents at one grocery store might cost $1.09 at another store twenty miles away. You can shop around for bargains, but that might cut into your fuel budget. Unless you're able to really sit down and cruise the internet to find deals at local stores and any relevant coupons, try to plan things out.

You might notice that we included "expenses from home." For some van dwellers, it's impossible to break a lease or sell property in time to get on the road. Some actually maintain their homes, so they have a "base" to return to from time to time. They might have a tenant renting the home or sublease an apartment. If you choose to maintain a stationary home, there will be expenses associated with that location — a mortgage in your name, bills, etc. You'll definitely not want any unpleasant financial surprises while you're on the road, so be sure that you factor in those regular payments if you will have them.

There are also things you can stock up on beforehand, to some extent and expenses that you will only encounter at the start of your trip, and perhaps rarely afterward. Let's take a look at what those might look like.

Expense Category	Considerations	Your Calculation
Emergency Supplies	Storage bin Tarps Bungee cords Duct tape Road flares Jumper cables Tire patch kit Spare gas canister Jack Tool kit	
Camping/Outdoor Supplies	Storage bin Tent/equipment Backpacks Sleeping bags Flashlights/lanterns Batteries Multi-tool	
Health and Wellness	Mirror Tote for toiletries Scissors Towels Storage for dirty laundry	
Bedding	Pillows Sheets Variety of blankets Mattress/sleeping surface Storage for unused bedding	

Kitchen	Large container to store canned/boxed/dry food
Cooler or refrigerator
Small containers for open food/leftovers
Pots and pans
Cooking tools (spatula, serving spoons, can opener, bottle opener)
Eating utensils
Dishes
Burner or stovetop
Fuel for cooktop
Dish bin
Dishrags

Again, this is not a comprehensive list for every possible scenario, but a few helpful guidelines to get you thinking about what items are part of your necessary routine.

Many of these items will need replacing depending on the length of your trip, and in case there is any accidental damage. Overall these will not be things that need to be replaced weekly or even monthly.

Advice from the Road: Part 4

A word about storage.

Everything in your van will need a place to live. Everything.

One of the most challenging parts of living in a van is the fact that you can't put your dirty laundry on a chair and deal with it on laundry day. You can't just let the dishes hang out overnight in the sink. Your van will become very crowded, messy, stinky, and full of pests unless you stash your dirty laundry somewhere, keep your dishes clean and put away, and your surfaces tidy.

Worse yet, if you leave food sitting out, you run the risk of attracting bears, coyotes, wolves, and more. While not naturally aggressive, these critters are very interested in any tasty tidbits you might have onboard, and they're naturally equipped with the claws and jaws that will help them get what they want!

When we hit the road, we started with several large bins:

- *One for our emergency supplies, which we labeled the Oh S**t Kit*
- *One for the kitchen goods, which included dry foods and all of our kitchenwares*
- *One for our camping gear, so if it got wet or muddy, it wouldn't roll all over the van and make a mess*
- *One for our dirty laundry — trust me, you want something that seals, especially if you're going to be hiking ten miles a day!*

These were each 60 gallon "under the bed box"-style heavy duty bins with lockable lids, specifically chosen to fit under the sleeping area. We could reach under the bed at any time and slide out the bin we needed — which we could identify because they were labeled on all four sides. The labels weren't anything fancy; just a strip of duct tape with the "Kitchen," "Camp," and so on written in permanent marker.

Under the shelf where these large bins lived was a storage area accessed by smaller doors. This had been where the original owner stored his emergency kit. We chose to create 6-quart sized plastic bins with lids to place in this area. They fit perfectly through the small door, and that way, wouldn't roll around or require additional containment.

We each had two — I chose to make one my toiletry kit — I put my shampoo, conditioner, soap, toothpaste, toothbrush, and hairbrush in one bin. That way, whenever we stopped at a place that had showers or ran into a rest stop to brush our teeth and wash our faces, I didn't have to pick and juggle what I needed — just grab the box and go. And since it had a lid, I didn't have to worry about things falling out and getting lost. If you've ever had a toothbrush fall on a rest area floor, you know that sinking feeling in your stomach when you lose an important piece of equipment!

My second bin held what I considered my daily necessities: medication, a spare phone charger, hair ties, the muscle rub I put on at night, dry *shampoo, hand lotion, lip balm, sunburn cream, and my mobile TENS unit. I also had a small bottle of air freshener in there, for that "we really need to make today laundry day" vibe.*

When it comes to living in a van, space is at a premium. You don't want things rolling around while you're driving, and you don't want to search all over the place when you're looking for something. If you can create a storage solution for every major area of your daily life, you'll make life so much easier for yourself.

You just have to remember to put everything back where you found it!

Chapter 2: Sticking to It

Now that you have an idea of what your expenses are going to look like, you've got to put some guidelines in place to help you stick to this plan. You know yourself best of all, so if you feel like there will be some moments of excess — such as visiting your favorite theme park or splurging at a restaurant you've always wanted to visit — make sure you add these into your budget at the outset. Just like when you lived in a stationary home, you want to make sure you have as much control over your money as possible.

There are many things you can do to keep your budget low, but you'll have to do some research and planning to carry out these options.

For example, making your own food is going to be considerably less expensive than eating at restaurants several times a week. But, as mentioned in Advice from the Road: Part 3, you'll need to be adequately prepared. Living on ramen every night is neither enjoyable nor nutritious. Make sure you incorporate methods for storing canned, boxed, and dry food, as well as produce, proteins, juices, leftovers, and other things that need to be kept chilled. This way, you'll be able to create healthful, tempting, budget-friendly meals without wasting food. We'll provide some tips on this topic in a later chapter.

Another place where you can save loads of money is by scouting out free parking and camping. Your online van community is possibly the best resource for finding a free place to catch some rest with travelers sharing some of their favorite spots for anyone who is currently on the road.

While there is nothing wrong with pulling into a paid campsite for the night, it can start to eat away at your budget. Many campsites require a $20-$40 per night camping fee, and if they have any extra perks, like vault toilets, WiFi, electricity, water hookups, laundry, or showers, there might be an additional fee to use those services.

Whenever possible, consider finding free camping. In the United States, National forests and wildlife areas and land owned by the Bureau of Land Management, they welcome free camping — as long as the land isn't privately owned. You'll need to do your homework in order to discover these spots, however, and there are several areas where there simply aren't public lands. We've included a few links in the **resource section** to guide your search.

Staying Green is another way to keep expenses down. This includes things like choosing reusable rags over paper products. Using as little water as possible for cleaning and reusing your greywater in practical ways or other options. If you use a generator, consider running it as little as possible. Try solar-powered flashlights — they can charge in the sunshine on your dashboard during the day and light up the van at night. If you don't need to be in motion, stay parked.

Anything you can do yourself saves you an expense, too. This includes maintenance and repair of nearly everything that's in your van or skoolie. If you can learn to perform minor mechanical repairs, you'll only need to pay for parts. If you can repair your own clothing, you won't need to replace it. If you have a roof rack and a sunny day, perhaps you save your quarters on a dryer and air dry your laundry.

Lastly, it's not a bad idea to sign up for fuel perks or discount programs, especially at national chains. Fuel is going to be a constant expense, and if you have the ability to earn discounts, you'll certainly be able to take advantage of them. You might also choose a credit card program through a gas station that provides discounts on fuels and products purchased from that chain. You may also stock up on gift cards for particular gas stations — some of them offer heavy discounts if you purchase gift cards in bulk. Investigate all of your opportunities to save on fuel, since you'll have absolutely no way of predicting what a gallon of gas will cost from one day to another!

Chapter 3: Earning Income While on the Move

If Van Life is to become your full-time lifestyle, you'll need either a very large amount of money before you hit the road, or you'll need regular income. More and more van dwellers are choosing to work while they're on the move. This can take on many shapes.

1. After completely rehabbing and rebuilding a van, you might find you're rather handy. Whenever money runs low, you go into a town, advertise as doing handy jobs, and make a few bucks.

2. You keep going until your funds drop below a certain limit. At that point, you pull into a semi-permanent camp park and get a job in town for a few months. You continue to live in your van, but you show up at the worksite, put in your hours, and let the income accumulate until you reach a comfortable spot where you can pick up and start driving again.

3. You keep your current job and work from the road. Many corporate-type jobs are allowing employees to telecommute from home or other alternative work environments. Your employer might require you to be signed on or otherwise reachable by phone and email during certain times of certain days, so you'll

need to plan wisely to have a reliable WiFi and phone signal during those times.
4. Freelancing is another career path that is gaining in popularity. Again, you'll need a fairly continuous WiFi signal and phone connection, but if you have a talent, you might check popular contracting sites for jobs you can accomplish anywhere you choose to be.
5. The Internet. We live in an age where you can get paid for talking about yourself on the internet. If you're a talented writer, photographer, videographer, or have the gift of gab, you can consider blogging, a YouTube channel, or a podcast. You'll have the ability to charge for ad space and make money by posting sponsored ads.

There are, of course, other types of income opportunities, but the main purpose of these examples is to help you appreciate that you don't have to be a trust fund baby or have millions in the bank before you hit the road.

Depending on the lifestyle you hope to lead, the compromises you're willing to make, and the skills you're willing to learn, anyone can hit the road at any time. It's just a matter of making sure you're very prepared for all of the possibilities and realities.

Advice from the Road: Part 5
I actually started my freelancing career from the road. Because I didn't want to spend the time and effort of sending all of my friends and family post-cards, I started a blog. As I was blogging, my friends would read about my adventures and share the link with their friends, and so on.

After a while, I started getting contacted by people who liked my writing style. They would have little writing projects they needed help with, and would I mind helping them out for a few bucks? Soon, I was devoting about an hour a day to these road projects.

I didn't plan to make money while on the road, but WiFi, Google Docs, PayPal, and the like make it super easy to gain a few bucks here and there. It wasn't long before I realized this was a real passion of mine, too!

Section 4: Preparing for Your Trip

We've discussed some of the preparations in earlier sections, but this one is designed to help you get really road ready. From this section you'll be able to not only make a checklist of things to pack but have places to pack them, and an orderly system for loading and unloading everything you've got. Furthermore, when things go sideways, you'll be prepared with alternatives!

Chapter 1: Your Utilities

When you were building or buying your van or skoolie, you made some very important decisions about things like power, water, toilets, showers, and more. Here is where you make sure you're ready to hit the road with all of these things!

For your power supply, both generators and solar power have special considerations. Do you have all of the knowledge and necessities to keep your generator in good, functioning order? What is your plan for running your generator? What happens if your generator goes out? You should always have a backup plan, such as flashlights and meals that don't require heating (or a heating source that doesn't require power). Does your toilet run off the generator? That's another possibility you'll need to consider.

Where are you going to get your water? Where are you going to dispose of your greywater? What if you run out of water? What are you going to store your water in? What happens if that storage tank gets damaged?

Much like you probably have a plan at home for what to do if the power goes out or a sewer main breaks, you'll need similar alternatives when you're on the road. At the same time, your storage space will be at a premium, so whatever you choose must be as simple as possible. If you are traveling with a family, for example, perhaps the path of least resistance is checking into a hotel for the night while you repair and re-sort all of the equipment that needs attention. If you're on your own, perhaps you stay put for the night, pitch a tent, and make the most of the situation.

Chapter 2: Sleeping Arrangements

When you were building your van or buying your van, you designated space for sleeping. Now that you've built your nest, it's time to feather it!

Your bed is actually a very important part of the van life experience. After all, if you sleep poorly, you might experience unnecessary back and neck pain, or become tired more easily, or just feel generally foggy and groggy. None of these are helpful when you are supposed to be driving or having adventures.

At the same time, it's generally not practical to have a king-sized thermal adjustable massaging bed installed in your van! Thankfully, there are plenty of options on the market when it comes to creating a sleeping environment that will be comfortable for you.

Start with a solid, flat, even base. Then add a mattress layer. Because you're working in a van, you might not be able to just wander into a mattress store and grab a standard commercial mattress. Instead, you might have to do some tailoring.

Futon mattresses tend to be a great medium for the base of your mattress layer. They're designed to be rolled up or folded, so if you need to stash your bedding while you drive, a futon mattress will not be offended. They're also typically stuffed with foam or padding. This means that if you cut into one to make it the right size, you can always just adjust the dimensions of the stuffing and sew it back up. Yes, this will require a little sewing skill, but it doesn't necessarily have to be gorgeous — just rugged and functional.

One thing to keep in mind with this type of mattress is that it isn't necessarily intended to be slept on every night for long periods of time. Do your research as you shop to find one that will be durable, and take care to flip and rotate your mattress often to ensure it wears evenly.

Another option is an inflatable mattress. If you need to use your sleeping area for other functions during the day, an inflatable mattress can be deflated and stashed in a relatively small area. The only downsides to this is that you will need to re-inflate it every time you use it, and it is possible for an air mattress to get tiny rips and holes that will need to be repaired in order for you to continue using it. Furthermore, you'll need to make sure the mattress fits within the dimensions of your sleeping area. Still, there are some very sturdy and comfortable air mattresses available.

On top of the mattress layer, you can add a variety of orthopedic and temperature regulating pads, which are available at most department stores and discount stores. A simple "egg-crate"-style pad might do the job, or you might want to find something that's more sturdy, firm, and will balance out your mattress. Make sure the padding you choose can be sized to your mattress, and if you're going to roll it up and store it when it's not in use, make sure it doesn't create too much unnecessary bulk. Some of the padding on the market might be as thick (or thicker!) than your mattress which could cause storage issues.

You might also consider getting what is affectionately termed a "bug bag" if you choose a non-inflatable mattress, especially if you plan to spend a lot of time in the true wilderness. This is a waterproof, insect-proof, crumb-proof mattress cover, which typically zips to keep the mattress truly protected from all of the elements. This might seem like an unnecessary extravagance until you knock over your water bottle onto your bed in the dark or find a swarm of ants casually enjoying a crumb of food you didn't realize you dropped. If you tailor your mattress to fit the space, it might not be a perfect fit, so buy a size bigger than whatever your mattress started as. You can always use bands or clips to keep it from rustling around as you sleep. Additionally, you'll be able to store your rolled-up mattress and pad in this if necessary.

Next comes the bed sheets and linens. Go with what makes you comfortable, but doesn't require a ridiculous amount of storage. You might see glorious social media pictures of van beds stacked with throw pillows. If you need throw pillows to be physically or mentally comfortable — get them. For the most part, however, you'll need enough pillows to keep your body comfortable, a fitted sheet to keep everything together, and some assortment of blankets for your preferred sleeping temperature.

Keep in mind that temperature can be a hard thing to regulate in a van, especially if you will not have a power source. You may choose to use your sleeping bag in colder climates, or if you're going to be in hotter locations, a light sheet or nothing at all. If you enjoy sleeping with a comforter in a climate-controlled house with a fan blasting directly at you, your sleeping situation might change once you're on the road.

This is another scenario where doing a test run in your garage, basement, or corner of a room will be a good idea. Set up your mattress, pad, and all the accessories you'd like to try. See how it feels, and adjust as necessary. This way, when you finally get out on the road, you'll be in a comfortable, familiar bed.

Remember also that your sheets and blankets will have to hang out in your van. Eventually, they will need to be washed and changed. You might want to have a spare set of sheets on hand and put the used sheets in with the dirty laundry. The goal is to be minimalist, but you need to be practical, as well. If you're the type of person who can wash and dry their sheets as necessary, then you'll be able to get away with just one set.

If you do choose to bring extra bedding, make sure you store it in a sealed container or bag. If you plan on going on any outdoor adventures, you will find that mud, sand, dirt, rocks, and snow will get everywhere. Make sure your clean linen stays clean until you're ready to use it by keeping it stowed away.

Another thing to consider when it comes to sleeping and bedding is windows. Yes, windows.

If you have a skoolie, you may have a lot of windows. That can be a huge advantage because you can open them at night and let the soft night air cool you while you sleep. In addition to the night air, however, you'll also let in the insects, pollen, falling leaves and seed pods, small intelligent rodents, and any looky-loos who might want to peep the interior of your home. All of these are incredibly irritating.

For windows that you'd like to keep open, you'll want to consider screens. You might have to make these yourself. Buy the kits for this at hardware stores. The best part is they don't take much work. You'll have to decide if you want to permanently install the screens or fashion them so they can be popped in when the windows are open. The second option is going to be most convenient, but less secure. A particularly clever rodent or curious person could figure out how to pop them right back out.

What about privacy windows? If you're living in a van, it's highly likely that you have a large rear window. Tinting it for privacy is possible, but be warned that different states have different laws on how dark windows can be. Instead, you might wish to fashion a privacy curtain that can be pulled across the window at night. You can install an actual curtain or use Velcro strips adhered around the van window to hang a blanket or other fabric across the window.

When thinking about window covering, remember that anything you have in the van will get dusty and dirty (maybe even smelly!). The insides of your windows will also gather condensation from your breath as you sleep on cool nights, so make sure your window treatments aren't going to be spoiled by getting slightly damp.

Your main goals for creating your sleep setting will be comfort, climate, the ability to stow and set up quickly and easily, cleanliness, and a sense of privacy. Together, these elements can't necessarily guarantee you a perfect night of sleep, but they'll certainly help!

Advice from the Road: Part 6

The first night in our van, I imagined that everyone was looking in on me. I tried to hide with the blankets over my head, but it was so hot. Eventually, I started feeling more and more comfortable with leaving the windows cracked, and then fully open.

That's when the mosquitos came out. Great big, blood-sucking mosquitos. The van was absolutely filled with them, buzzing all night, feasting on our faces. Even in the mountains, where there was snow, they still came to visit.

We quickly put up makeshift screens in the windows, but it wasn't long before the bugs found all the holes. Our next investment was perfectly-sized screens, which we affixed to the window frame with large, industrial-strength Velcro strips. The screens stowed neatly behind the driver's seat, and extra Velcro is an easy investment.

The result was a quiet night of sleep with peaceful mountain breezes and no bug attacks!

Chapter 3: Storage Solutions

Much like power sources, storage solutions are something we've touched on several times already. As you prepare to hit the road, it's crucial to really get everything organized and accounted for.

As you pack, you'll find that there might be a few things that you don't quite have a spot for. This happens to every single person as they pack up for their maiden voyage. It is highly likely that you will overpack due to "The Unknown," which will leave you scrambling for space.

Many of us pack like we're fleeing quickly, but the good news about gearing up for your new life in a van is that you have time to be strategic and plan what you pack.

Clothing

When it comes to clothing, you're probably thinking you'll need a few daytime outfits, something comfortable to wear while driving, stuff to hike and do other outdoor activities in, and probably something civilized to wear if you decide to go out to a restaurant, museum, or other "citified" location.

It's important to note that most clothing can do a lot of work in between washings. The jeans you wear while driving might be perfectly fine for touring a local art museum. The leggings you wear while hiking through a National Park might do the trick for driving long distances the next day.

That's not to say that clothing won't get soiled or damaged and need immediate laundry or replacement, but it's unlikely that you'll need to prepare with four pairs of pants per day. Instead, plan to hand wash anything that needs immediate attention (which you can handle in your dish tub — making the most out of everything!).

If you plan to do a lot of outdoor activities, you will want to make sure you pack plenty of clean, appropriate socks and the correct footwear. You might find yourself packing more pairs of shoes than pairs of jeans, depending on what your trip has in store for you. Hiking, running, canoeing, rock climbing or caving, and water sports all require different types of footwear, as well as storage options that can contain mud, dirt, water, and odor.

Additionally, you'll need to make sure you've got climate-related gear. Fleece jackets, water-proof windbreakers, swimsuits, and even sweaters or sweatshirts might be a great thing to pack. Just remember — you don't need to bring ALL of them.

If you're the type to overpack for a vacation, start by pulling everything you want to take with you out of the drawers and closets. Then reduce that by half. Then reduce by half again. Keep paring down until you have about seven to ten days of clothing options. You might want to check out the Capsule Wardrobe method and apply this to your overall wardrobe selection. Your goal is to carry less but to have more options.

You can always wash your clothes. You can always buy something on the road if a particular need arises. But once you're on the road, the only way to get rid of things you want to keep is to pack them up and ship them to someone who will store them for you!

Supplies

And then you've got all of your supplies. This can range from your breakdown kit to your pots and pans, to your toiletries, and so on.

If you've got built-in cabinetry, that's going to solve a lot of problems. At the same time, remember that your van or skoolie is going to be in motion. That means braking, accelerating, hard turns, winding roads, bumps, and potholes. The objects in your cabinets will shift and move, which can make a mess, or leave a bump on your head in the case of overhead bins.

Many van dwellers like to create storage solutions that prevent things from moving around too much while the van is in motion. One way to do this is to group items in plastic bins. Bins with lids can be especially helpful when it comes to making sure vital supplies don't escape and roll around while you're driving. There are also rack-style shelving solutions that can be installed in cabinets that help keep things stable. Velcro, magnets, bungee-style cords, tie-downs, and more are all very helpful resources in keeping things in place during transit, too.

If you do use bins, it's a good idea to keep them all labeled or color-coded for easy access. Additionally, make sure certain items can be accessed inside or outside the van. It's unlikely that you'll want to open the rear door and stand in the pouring rain to find a can opener.

Anything you can do to make the contents of your van stable and accessible will go a long way toward extending the comfort and usability of your van's contents. For the most part, this will take practice. Things that seem to make sense before you hit the road might take a different shape once you get used to the overall flow of van living.

Chapter 4: Emergency Kit

When you think of an "Emergency Kit," the first thing that probably comes to mind is a first aid kit. A first aid kit is an absolute necessity, but the emergency kit includes so much more. After all, you're preparing for unplanned events in a home that's on wheels, powered by many moving mechanical parts.

When thinking about what to put in your emergency kit, first consider the relatively common incidents that might occur to a motor vehicle. For example, flat tires. If you're driving a large transit bus, you're not going to be able to just head over to the shoulder and pop the spare on. But for smaller vans, a spare tire, jack, and tire iron are a great idea. You might even bring a tire patch kit, in the event of minor issues that can be addressed shortly at a tire shop.

What about jumper cables or a battery jump kit? Many of the older vans don't include automatic headlights or even an annoying buzz or beep to let you know you've left your lights on. You don't want to be stuck in the middle of nowhere, with no cell phone signal and no battery power.

A fire extinguisher is a very important addition to any emergency kit. Depending on the size of your vehicle, you might want to bring a few along, for the inside of the vehicle and for the vehicle itself. While a fire is unlikely, it is possible. And if you're planning to brave the wilderness? You might not be within easy access of emergency services.

A tarp may seem unnecessary. After all, vans and buses have roofs, and they're pretty leak proof. The issue is the windows. Glass is prone to cracks and breakage, and having water streaming through the inside of your van is no one's idea of a good time. While a tarp and duct tape aren't a permanent fix, they will help take care of the issue while you create a plan. Tarps also make a pretty handy landing pad, tent base, canopy for lounging outside, "spare room," and more. If you're using an outdoor hanging shower, you can use the tarp as your "floor" so you don't have to stand in mud. The uses go on and on, making a pretty convincing argument for having a tarp on hand... just in case!

Battery-operated lighting is also a good idea. This can take the form of flashlights, small lanterns, and more. Don't rely on your cell phone flashlight as a light source. If you find yourself without power and need light for a lengthy period of time, using your phone flashlight will just drain the battery. Instead, save that battery, and use a device that doesn't have the ability to call for help! Make sure you pack spare batteries as well — don't assume that you'll be able to get more whenever you need them. Batteries take up very little room and are worth it to not find yourself in a dark and scary situation.

Solar flashlights and lanterns are also fine options — just make sure you let them see the sun during the day, so they're charged when you need them.

Depending on where you're going to spend your time, you might want an emergency water purification kit on hand. While you'll largely be able to plan ahead to manage your water supply, you might find yourself in a dry location with a leak. Being able to instantly replenish your water supply is a huge benefit, no matter where you are, or what type of adventure you're having. If you're relying on a fixed freshwater tank, make sure you have a backup plan. That can even mean having a few gallons of drinking water from the grocery store on hand — just make sure you've got them stashed away in a safe location, where they can't move around and possibly spring a leak while you're driving!

Having a spare gasoline can onboard can also be helpful, especially if you're going to be traveling through long stretches of uninhabited territory. The most important consideration for having gasoline onboard is storing it properly, so it doesn't tip and spill, become too hot or too cold, or accidentally release harmful fumes into the cabin. If you have children or pets with you, you'll want to be absolutely certain they can't accidentally come in contact with the gasoline directly, either.

If you've learned some of the basics of vehicle maintenance, you'll want to have a toolset onboard also. Generally speaking, this will include a hammer or mallet, and the right-sized wrenches for all of the pieces and parts within your vehicle. You might also want a screwdriver that fits the interior screws, just in case something works loose. First-time van dwellers are always a bit surprised at what things work loose when traveling consistently over bumpy roads! There's no need to take any tools that have no use in your vehicle, so make sure you pack wisely and organize well. A small toolbox or carrying case will save you tons of frustration when you're already upset about a breakdown.

Other helpful things to have onboard are items that have plenty of practical uses. Duct tape is almost always helpful for one reason or another. From temporarily taping the soles back onto your shoes, to holding a loose cabinet door down until you can fix it, to waterproofing a baseball cap, nearly every van dweller has some zany story involving duct tape coming to the rescue in a pinch. Make sure you invest in the truly waterproof, truly sticky stuff, too.

Multi-tools, such as Leatherman or Swiss Army Knives, will prove useful in a variety of situations, as well. You'll be thrilled to have one of these in your kit when you lose the nail clippers, need to cut something to size, try to open a bottle... the list goes on and on. A pocket-sized utensil with nearly infinite uses is always welcome in a van.

Matches or a long grill-style lighter can also be helpful. If you have a propane stove or burner that you'll be using, these will be a necessity, as well as if you plan on regularly building campfires. Even if you don't plan on needing to start a fire, you might find yourself in need of a heat and light resource if you lose your power source. Camping matches are a small easy-to-store investment that could really come in handy in a pinch.

In some cases, you'll want to pack several of these items. If, for example, you're a whole family on the road, you'll probably want several flashlights, which means stocking up on more batteries. If you're going to be gone for a significant amount of time, it can't hurt to have two rolls of duct tape

— one in the cabin, and one on reserve with the vehicle maintenance equipment.

Now the tricky part — where do you put all of this stuff? With the exception of items that need special storage considerations, like gasoline and water, you might choose to put everything together in a tote or cabinet that is exclusively designated for your emergency kit. However, you might want to keep some of the smaller items in an easy-to-reach spot, like the glove box, or a small in-cabin kit that can be accessed quickly. After all, it makes no sense to have a flashlight if you have to fumble around in the dark in order to find it.

When it comes to emergency supplies, there's a fine line between "too prepared" and "possible catastrophe." Just like in a stationary home, it's impossible to prepare for every eventuality. It may seem even more challenging to think of all the dangers that might befall you on the road. In order to give yourself more peace of mind, do some research beforehand on the areas where you'll be traveling. What types of perils have other van dwellers encountered? Do other travelers have recommendations for supplies to have on hand? Knowing what others have experienced in that area can help give you some perspective on your own needs so you can plan ahead.

Chapter 5: Food

The topic of food has come up several times, and for good reason — we literally cannot live without it. In our stationary worlds, we pop into the grocery store whenever we need to and load up on fresh produce, meats, cheese, eggs, frozen foods, and so on. We bring them home, organize them in our full-sized refrigerators, freezers, and cabinets, and plan to use them before the expiration date. Sometimes we don't feel like cooking, so we head out to a restaurant or order delivery, and if we order too much food, we throw that in the refrigerator and reheat it in our microwaves the next day.

It is technically still possible to do all of that in a van or bus, as long as you've got the space, power, and equipment to do so. You may not have full-sized appliances and cabinets, but you can incorporate smaller, camper-style units that do the same job. This is a very good idea if you'll be traveling with children, or if you're making a van living your permanent lifestyle.

For many Van Lifers, though, there is neither room nor practical need for appliances. In reality, none of the traditional kitchen appliances are required to live. An economical use of food products, a cold storage option, and the ability to heat food and water are really all it takes to keep yourself fed on the road.

As mentioned earlier, coolers are very helpful. The type of cooler you choose does have some bearing on your food options and usage, however. An ice-chest type cooler is typically very inexpensive, and melted ice can be recycled as bathwater or used for cleaning up certain non-food items (like the floor of the van, your muddy flip-flops, etc.). The downside to this is that your cooler will fill with water as the ice melts. Unless it is replenished regularly, that means that anything in the cooler can get water-logged, and anything that gets too warm has a chance of spoiling. But, if you practice extreme discipline in the use of your ice chest, there's no reason why this can't work.

Plug-in coolers can be very helpful, too. They are generally more expensive than ice chests, but you have the luxury of never worrying about the ice/water ratio. At the same time, you've got to have the power supply to keep it going. Most units require 12 volts of power, which isn't unreasonable. If you've got an older van with no power supply, however, you might be wary of leaving it plugged in overnight, as it might drain the battery. Some coolers will have the ability to keep their contents cooled if unplugged for short periods, and some will not. Food poisoning while on the road is even more uncomfortable than it is in a house or apartment, so don't tempt the fates when it comes to food safety. Make sure your food is stored at the appropriate temperature — if your cooler can't handle it, don't take the risk.
When it comes to storing produce, you have two main goals. The first is

to not have it rolling around the cabin as you drive, and the second is to not attract insects or other wildlife that might be interested in sampling your meals. Generally speaking, the cooler is a fine place to keep your fruits and veggies, even if you wouldn't technically put a particular item there at home.

As for dry foods, the goals are the same as produce, only you won't necessarily want to stash everything in the cooler. Food-safe plastic storage tubs are a very good idea for things like rice and noodles and grains, as they keep the bugs out and all of the food in one place. Canned goods and other self-storing foods(like ramen noodle packets) only need to be stored in a way that they're secure and not rolling underfoot while you're trying to drive.

Snack foods and bread products are a different consideration on the road. At home, you might roll up the bag inside the cracker box, throw a chip-clip on a bag of crispy snacks, and just keep the bread shut with a twist-tie. On the road, you've got a greater exposure to insects, and living in an open-air type environment means things will go stale and grow mold more quickly. You've also got to consider curious wildlife, as well. Make sure you can tuck your snacks and bread products somewhere safe where they won't be shared without your permission.

If you're an avid camper or outdoor fan, you probably associate foods like peanut butter, trail mix, power bars, tuna, canned stew, and ramen with living outdoors. These are certainly staples of Van Life, as well, but you can diversify your diet. The key is making sure you use everything immediately, unless you have sufficient, reliable cold storage for leftovers.

When you go to the grocery store now, you might take advantage of sales, like 3 for $10 salad kits or "fill the freezer" meat deals. Without a ton of cold storage space, that's no longer going to make sense. Instead, you'll want to purchase only what you can eat or adequately store right now. That's not to say you can't have salad or meat but that you'll want to look at portions realistically to avoid waste.

Canned and dried food is always a go-to when it comes to living in a situation where there's not a lot of space, time, or refrigeration, but these foods are often high in sodium and preservatives. Make sure you're making wise choices for your body, health, and lifestyle. Good nutrition is key to giving you stamina and helping you maintain your health while you're on the road. Make sure you're fueling your body in a way that's appropriate for you.

When planning meals, you can always take advantage of what resources you have to create back-to-back meals that will meet the requirements of multiple food groups. For example, if you purchase one salad kit, one can of beans, a bell pepper, two tomatoes, and one large chicken breast, you can have a protein-packed chicken/bean chili for dinner with a tasty side salad, then follow it up with a big salad topped with chicken for lunch the next day. Simply cook the chicken first, then cut it into two portions — the amount you'll add to tonight's chili and the bit that you'll slice up for lunch tomorrow. Make sure you put what you're not using right away into the cooler immediately. Throw the beans, a chopped tomato, and half the bell pepper into a pot with the chicken and your favorite seasonings for a tasty "road chili." Make yourself a small salad to enjoy, too, and make sure you seal up the rest and store it in the cooler. Tomorrow, you can use the other half of the bell pepper, the second tomato, the rest of the salad kit, and the leftover chicken to have a nutritious salad.

This is just one example of how being strategic with your food and resources can help you avoid "camp food burnout." There are plenty of recipe guides for low tech and outdoor living, and we've included some links in the **resources** at the end of this book. You might feel now like having a cooler and a propane camp stove will be incredibly limiting, but the reality is that you can eat almost exactly like you do at home — you just have to scale back and be more realistic about your food use. Before you start your maiden voyage, you might want to keep track of what you cook, what you eat, how many leftovers you have, and how quickly you eat those leftovers. This will give you a little more insight about your food volume usage, so you can be more adequately prepared once you get on the road.

Section 5: Where Are You Going to Go?

Your van is fully packed. You're ready to go. You're equipped with all sorts of new and exciting knowledge.

So where do you go?

For some people, there's a very obvious destination in mind. Perhaps you've spent your life pining for a visit to a particular landmark, park, or museum. Naturally, you'll want to head there immediately. But the beauty of van living is that there are no destinations — only the amazing journey. Once you've hit your ideal spot — then what? You might be feeling a bit lost.

Other people might not have a clear destination selected. They might have a few general ideas of things they'd like to see, but they haven't really figured out where to go or how to get there.

Then there's a third party, which borrows a little from the first group and the second group. These folks have a definite list of things they want to see but look forward to connecting the dots with adventure.

There's plenty of grey area in between these three options, as well. If you're worried about feeling constricted by requiring plans, you'll be glad to know that there's really no wrong way to do your Van Life. It is your practice, your lifestyle, and we're just here to tap you on the shoulder and give you practical advice and suggestions. If you're the sort of person who needs guidance or help getting started, that's also not wrong. You're allowed to be confused and overwhelmed.

Let's take a look at a few different strategies that are popular among road warriors. If you're feeling too decisive, this might help you open your mind to more possibilities. If you're feeling too free, this can help you start to reach out and explore a few solid "x" marks to put on your map for future destinations.

The "Keep Moving" Strategy

Have you ever heard the phrase "goes as the wind blows?" There are van dwellers who truly do this. If they wake up and feel like checking out the west coast, so be it. Maybe the mountains next week. How about a forest?

Having a home on wheels really does mean you can go where you want, when you want, but remember that fuel costs are a very real thing. If you have an unlimited budget, perhaps driving in perpetual circles and constantly being on the move isn't a bad thing. For those who need to be aware of every cent they spend, perhaps a little bit of planning can help temper that possible spending.

Navigation is a necessary evil, even if you just want to wander. While getting lost can be fun, it does lose its novelty when bad things happen, and you don't know where you are. It can also wind up feeling a little unnecessary and uninspiring over time.

Ultimately, the "Keep Moving" strategy can turn up some wonderful roadside surprises that you never expected to find. These lifetime experiences can never be forced, anticipated, or replaced. There is so much beauty in this world, and having the freedom to experience all the beauty you can is something many people can't even imagine.

This method does require a bit of careful compromise between wandering and respecting your budget, as well as any needs you might have for bathing, laundry, and stocking up on supplies. There needs to be a bit of conscious planning but never so much that you feel restricted.

Long-Term Living

Other people like to have the opportunity to really experience the culture of a location, even if it's just for a temporary time period.

While you might stake a claim on a particular camping spot, either within a designated camp park or out in the wilderness, that doesn't mean you can't leave and explore. As discussed earlier, some van dwellers take along a scooter or bicycle, so they can leave the confines of the van to wander — you're only limited by how far you're willing to stray from the van in one day.

Much like wandering, there are both pros and cons to this type of adventure. You might end up spending more in camping fees, due to your long-term stay, but you'll likely save on your fuel budget. Even if you do your local exploration in your van, it's likely that you'll be staying within a 20-mile radius.

Additionally, you'll be familiar with the area and some of the local options. You'll establish a place to purchase groceries, do your laundry, and replenish supplies. You might find some local entertainment options that you'd never expect to experience. Locals are a great source of knowledge, input, and recommendations that you won't find anywhere else, so it might be worth it to hang out at the local watering hole and find out when the county fair is or what local band is playing soon.

At the same time, you might find yourself feeling just a little too cozy. You might start to think that you've given up one home and just moved somewhere else. Always remember — you have the freedom to start the engine and throw it into gear anytime you want. Just figure out the next place to go, and get those actual wheels in motion!

Connecting the Dots
One fun method of travel is to turn the whole experience into a wild game of "connect the dots." You can pick a handful of things you'd really like to do while you're on the road, then mosey from point to point.

There are no restrictions on this method. You choose your timeframe and how you get from Point A to Point B. The only limits that exist are those that you create. For example, if you want to go to a concert in a specific city on a specific day, you'll need to make sure you make appropriate travel plans. Otherwise, you have the freedom to wander, without the lack of direction. In many ways, this is the best of both worlds!

Advice from the Road: Part 7

Our trip started as a fifty-page list of things we wanted to see, categorized by state. Yes. You read that right — fifty pages. There was no possible way we were going to be able to squeeze everything in, and we knew that, but still, it seemed like a good way to start.

Our first step was to pull out a huge map of the United States, including major freeways. This map was really huge — it took up our entire dining room table.

Next, we used little dot stickers to plot out some of the places we wanted to go, state by state. We put everything on there. In some states, it looked absolutely ridiculous. In other states, it was clear that we had a concentration of interest in a specific area.

The plans started to take shape from there. We knew we had a limited timeframe for our first trip (if you can call a year "limited"), so we had to create a way to see as much as possible without being too indirect.

We made a few rules to make sure we kept with our desire to explore: First, we would limit our use of major freeways and take as many back roads as possible. Second, any time we stopped, we'd check out what was going on in a five-mile radius and see what we needed to check out before we kept moving on.

We cheated a little on both of those rules. We broke the "five-mile rule" a lot, and there were a few times when we were so tired, we decided to take the fastest route instead of the scenic route to make sure we were driving safely. Still, I have absolutely no regrets about the number of things we were able to see, do, and try, and the diversity of those experiences.

Section 6: Staying Happy on the Road

We started this book by guiding you through the Van Life mindset, to see if you're prepared for this undertaking. After all, creating an entirely new lifestyle from scratch is no small task! At this point, you've got your vehicle. It's packed. You're confidently armed with a variety of literature, including repair manuals, replacement part specs, maps, pamphlets, recipes, and so on.

You probably feel pretty well prepared for anything that could happen, and you really should feel confident with all you have accomplished up to this point. Van Life is not for the weak of heart, and preparing for life on the road is a serious rite of passage.

Still, there's really nothing that can prepare you for the feeling you'll get, sitting behind that giant steering wheel, listening to your engine complain as it climbs its first winding mountain road with you.

And there's also nothing quite like the feeling of lying awake at night, on your van mattress, wishing for the thick memory foam bed you had at home, where you can fall asleep to your favorite Netflix series without worrying about burning up the power supply, in air conditioning that you can crank when it gets hot, with a shower and a toilet that require little to no maintenance in the very next room. You might just find yourself longing for a place that doesn't kind of faintly smell like shoes and laundry all the time. That's ok! You're entirely allowed to have these feelings.

In this section, we'll focus on how to keep the motivation and feelings of well-being continuing even if life is starting to feel stale. While we can't cure your melancholy, we do want you to know that this is normal and happens to absolutely everyone.

Chapter 1: Avoiding Boredom

During particularly long hauls, you will likely experience boredom. Your first reaction to recognizing this boredom may be fear. You uprooted your entire life to live on the road, only to feel the same boredom you felt at home. What is wrong with you?

The answer? Nothing. You're allowed to feel stagnant, especially when you are.

The beauty of Van Life is that you can shake it up. Celebrate that you can go anywhere. If you start feeling like "all I do is drive, and I don't even like it," then go to a National Park. Hike the trails nobody hikes. Or, if you're feeling lonely, hike the trails that everyone hikes. Meet new trail buddies. Let yourself be in awe of the natural beauty that surrounds you.

If, at any time, you feel like you see the same stuff every day, you need to find some hidden gems to get you out of the rut. Hop on the internet. Go into a diner or dive bar and talk to the older locals. In your life at home, you could break out of a rut by calling your friends and doing something predictable, like meeting up for coffee or a movie or drinks. On the road, if you're feeling the monotony, you need to go meet Sue, the World's Largest Cow (or whatever is "cool and unusual" in your vicinity). Do an online search for "cool and unusual things" and a location, and you'll turn up loads of things you've never even heard about!

Find out what's going on at the local college. What bands are playing? What kind of lectures or exhibitions can you find? If nothing comes to mind, just park at the end of a street, any street, walk until you don't want to keep going, then walk back to your van. You might wonder what that will accomplish. Well, what are five things you saw during your walk that were interesting?

Keep yourself in the mindset that you have control over your exploration. Though not every place you wander will feature jaw-dropping scenery, activities that make your heart race, or experiences that open your soul, there will be plenty of things that will be new to you. Embrace these.

You'll also want to keep your mind engaged while you're on the road, with activities you can enjoy within the confines of the van. There will be bad weather days. You will probably get sick or injured. Or, you just might not feel like leaving the van on a particular day. Make sure you have plenty of stuff that will keep you engaged and entertained.

A few examples include:

- Audiobooks, music, and podcasts. You don't have to stop learning and growing, just because you're no longer a part of a wall-to-wall, brick-and-mortar society! Use this opportunity to expand your horizons. Choose audiobooks that teach you about totally new topics. Listen to performers you've only heard about from your friends. Check out podcasts that will challenge your thoughts and endear you to the human experience.
- Activity books. This may seem like it's geared to kids, but adults can gain a lot from coloring, doing logic puzzles, crosswords, sudoku, or even by trying to find Waldo! When you stare at the road for hours at a time, your mind craves something different, so put your creativity and problem-solving skills to the test with some harmless activities that won't require a lot of space or supplies.
- Blogging. Though a brief glimpse through the **resources section** may make it sound like the internet is already saturated with Van Life blogs, there's always room for your experience. You can start a blog for free and use it to share your pictures and thoughts with friends and family. You might also start a variety of social media platforms specifically for your voyage. If sharing these thoughts with the whole world isn't your style, old fashioned pen-and-paper journals are always an option.

Lastly, try to take a deep breath and remember to enjoy the moment. It is very easy for depression and anxiety to creep up on you when you're on the road, especially if you're alone. As you drive, you have lots of time to stop and reflect on negative thoughts. It's easier said than done, but don't let your mind trick you like that.

Come up with a mantra that reaffirms your abilities. You have made it this far. You have created a new lifestyle for yourself. You are doing just fine. Today is always an adventure, and you have opportunities on the road that many people will never take advantage of. Remind yourself to love what you're doing. Cherish every detail, every new experience, every little thing you've never seen before.

This is your dream, and you are making it come true.

Chapter 2: Homesickness/Loneliness

Being on the road can feel very lonely sometimes. Most of us are used to living a more sedentary lifestyle or one where we can just pick up the phone and text or call our friends. You and your buddies probably get together now and then to catch up, have dinner, watch movies, and just generally hang out. It's different when you're on the road.

You can still have friends over to your van, of course, but now you have to meet new people. You'll probably visit friends and family that you don't usually get to see while you're traveling, but all the people you see every day will be exactly where you left them.

While this concept might make you feel very sad, that's not entirely bad news. They're exactly where you left them. You can go visit them. Some people feel that, since they're devoted to Van Life now, they can't go home. It's ok to go home.

There is going to come a time when both your body and soul will long for the comforts and conveniences of home. If you have the desire to go back to the place where you started your journey, go for it! Stay with friends or family back in your hometown. Go to your regular haunts. Everyone will want to hear stories, so share them! Soon, your heart will long for the road again, and off you'll go, spiritually refreshed from your visit.

You might also try planting for a bit wherever you are on the road. Find a long-term parking solution, and let yourself have a routine for a few days. Sometimes the brain and body need a sense of regularity and stability to help you put everything into perspective.

Additionally, keep your finger on the pulse of the van community. There are plenty of meetups scheduled throughout the year, even around the world. You might start conversing with your new best friends via the forums, blogs, and social media sites dedicated to those living the Van Life. Becoming a part of a community can help you with those feelings of longing and belonging.

Advice from the Road: Part 8
The first time you miss an important family event, it will break your heart. You'll see the pictures online — maybe your whole family enjoying cake together — and you'll wish you were there. You'll be able to feel all the hugs, hear the laughter, smell the over-cooked casserole, and your heart will cry out.

The first event I missed was my niece's birthday party. It was a small shindig, and really not a big deal, but when I saw the pictures of her opening her gifts, beaming at the camera, surrounded by torn wrapping paper and the bounty of her party, I cried. I wanted to be there. But it wasn't practical to be there and here, 800 miles away in the middle of the mountains.

Sometimes, you'll feel like you've done something selfish. People will try to tell you that, too. But the reality is that we all choose the lifestyle that's best for us.

You can choose to come home for the holidays, the birthdays, the anniversaries, the bachelorette parties, and so on. But the realities of time and space mean that you can't be in two places at once. You can't summit Angel's Landing and be in Florida by dinner time.

Remember that you can make room for everything and anything that you value, but you don't have to make room for everything and anything that's suggested to you. You can always go back. You can always come back. Don't let yourself feel rushed or pushed.

One tool that I began to value from the road was phone calls. It's so easy to get away with texting conversations, but when you're on the road, hearing someone's voice can be very soothing. It's also likely that there's someone who wants to hear from you, too. When you have a fully-charged battery and service, reach out — make a call. Talk. It'll do your soul some good.

Chapter 3: Housekeeping

Housekeeping might not be the most enjoyable use of time, but it's extremely necessary. If you're the type who has a "junk drawer," a "mail folder," or "a laundry chair". You might find Van Life challenging at first.

In a van, any mess you make is proportionately larger than it would be in a house or apartment. If you leave a pair of shoes on the floor of your bedroom, you can probably maneuver around them pretty easily. If you leave your shoes on the floor of your van, you will trip over them, and you will get mad at yourself for leaving them where you could trip over them.

Living in close quarters requires a new level of hygiene, which can be especially tricky when you don't have the ability to give yourself hour-long exfoliating showers every day. Keeping the stinky things stored, as we mentioned earlier, is a great way to prevent a long-term, permanent reek, but you'll still need to wash everything regularly. That includes yourself, your laundry, your bed linens, any rugs you might have, your dishes, and your commode, just to name a few. Make sure you dispose of spoiled food immediately. If you are practicing recycling on the road, make sure your empties are rinsed.

Not only do these practices cut down on bad smells, but they also cut down on bugs and critters. Wildlife is a very real part of Van Life and can include everything from the innocuous visits of birds, squirrels, and chipmunks, to the possibly dangerous curiosity of bears. You'll definitely want to avoid the headache of an ant infestation, but there's no reason to tempt a hungry grizzly!

To avoid all of this, make sure you sweep your abode on wheels regularly. Clean up any spills immediately. Get rid of trash as frequently as you can. Do your part to keep things as clean as possible.

Not only does this practice have sanitary implications, but it can also make you feel better about your dwelling. Some people feel a sense of purpose and pride when they mow their lawn or scrub their floors in a stationary home. Doing something as simple as washing all of the mud from your latest off-road excursion can remind you that you love your new home and your new life, and you wouldn't have it any other way!

In Conclusion

Is Van Life for everyone? No. The truth is that most people won't even consider, think about, or be able to fathom the idea of living in a small, mobile space. The idea of not knowing where you're going to sleep tonight, or heating up beans over a propane burner in the dark, or going to the bathroom outside at midnight might sound like an absolute nightmare to some people.

But there is a special breed of people. There are some who hear or read phrases like this, and their hearts beat a little faster and a little harder. The ideas of "opportunities" and "unknowns" sound more welcoming than fearsome. They look at the walls around them and feel like they're being crushed by stability. These are the people who are born Van Lifers.

Are you one of them? Only you can tell for sure. If there is one thing we hope you've learned from this book, it's that you can't do Van Life the wrong way. Beyond that, building your own Van Life is a process and not one that comes quickly or easily.

Can you find "any old" van, start the engine, and take off? Sure! There are some people who are naturally adaptive. But for those of us who are taking off from what feels like a very sheltered spot, there can be lots of planning and attention to details in order to feel more secure about this huge decision.

If there's one piece of advice all van dwellers should know, it's "Don't panic when things go wrong — they just will." The first time things go topsy-turvy, it will be terrifying. There will be setbacks. You will revisit the drawing board many times. The good news is that, even when things go upside down, they tend to put themselves right sideup again, as long as you don't panic.

Remember also that this isn't a competition. Just because someone on social media does it differently, doesn't mean you've failed. If you catch a cold and spend two days in a hotel recovering, that doesn't mean you're inadequate. It means you did the best thing you could for yourself in that situation. If you choose to start the day with your favorite chain restaurant doughnut and coffee, don't feel like your experience is any less authentic than the bloggers who figure out how to make overnight oats in a tin coffee mug. Just make sure you budget for the expense and get on with your best Van Life.

In short, be sure to enjoy every step of the journey. You are doing something many people dream of, but very few people get to experience.

This is the beginning of your new life.

Section 7: Helpful Resources for Future Van Dwellers

The following links lead to online blogs, reference materials, and websites that can help you with every step of the process of converting to Van Life. The views and ideas expressed in each of these links belong solely to the person writing it, so please don't consider their inclusion an endorsement or partnership. We simply wanted to get you started on the quest for more information.

Remember, there is no "wrong" way to do Van Life. There are only ways that work better for your lifestyle and things that don't work for you. It's a very personal experience that often requires a lot of trial and error.

Still, sometimes it helps to read the experiences of those who have tried it, are doing it, or are in the same position as you are when it comes to trying something very, very different.

Feel free to check out some of these links to draw inspiration, and continue your quest for more information!

The Van Life State of Mind:
As noted, you've got to be in the right headspace to really enjoy the wild ride.

http://www.alwaystheroad.com/blog/2017/3/24/is-van-life-for-you-how-to-know_if_its_right-for-you

Parking Options, Camping Options, and Sleep Spots
Tracking down a spot where you can catch up on some rest or spend the night can be challenging, especially when you're on a tight budget. Here are some resources to help you find a safe, practical place to rest.

https://www.campendium.com/camping/vanlife/
http://thevanual.com/sleeping-and-safety/

https://www.cheaprvliving.com/stealth-city-parking/bobs-12-commandments-for-stealth-parking-in-the-city/
https://divineontheroad.com/overnight-parking/
https://kombilife.com/van-life-free-camping/
https://www.classicvans.com/
https://www.youtube.com/watch?v=oqPiP2JYVNc
https://www.nps.gov/index.htm

Choosing a Van

If the topic of vans as a vehicle is new to you, you'll definitely want to do additional research before starting the shopping process. Here are a few sites that will help you learn more about the types of vans and buses, as well as a variety of opinions to help guide you through the pros and cons of every option out there.

https://www.curbed.com/2018/1/31/16951486/best-van-conversion-rv-camper-vanlife
https://vanclan.co/best-van-to-live-in/
https://gnomadhome.com/why-choose-conversion-van-for-vanlife/
https://gearmoose.com/van-life-best-camper-vans/
https://weretherussos.com/van-chassis-camper-van-conversion/

Classic Van Lifers

As mentioned, Classic vans have a following of their own. Here are some links to resources for people who are living the "old school" way, with vans from earlier eras. Check out their thoughts, experiences, and words of advice.

https://bearfoottheory.com/category/van-life/
https://blog.feedspot.com/van_life_blogs/
https://vanclan.co/vanlife-blogs/

Skoolies

For those who are interested in larger format on-the-road living, buses are the way to go. The conversion, rehab, remodel, and updating of these vehicles could be a book on their own, so we've included a few links to folks who have gone through the process. Their insights, advice, trials, and tribulations can be helpful as you adjust to the learning curve of a great big diesel vehicle!

https://gearjunkie.com/school-bus-rv-camper-conversion-remodel
https://www.curbed.com/2019/3/6/18246221/camper-conversion-skoolie-vanlife-tiny-house
https://www.buslifeadventure.com/index.php/blog/16-blog/198-bus-life-vs-van-life-as-seen-through-the-eyes-of-a-van-dweller

The Cost of Van Living

While we've included some details about how to calculate your van shopping budget, your remodeling budget, your road budget, your overall experience budget and more, we can't predict all of the expenses that might go into your individual experience. Check out these resources for more inspiration.

https://www.moneyunder30.com/van-living
https://www.parkedinparadise.com/van-life-cost/
https://mymoneywizard.com/living-in-a-van/
https://www.explorist.life/how-much-does-van-life-cost/
https://faroutride.com/vanlife-actual-cost/

Generating Revenue on the Road

Again, we all need to follow our own path when it comes to careers, so only try this at home if you think you can make it work with your own skills, talents, and preferences. If you're feeling hesitant about trying to make a career work on the road, here are some thoughts, ideas, and words of wisdom from those who have made it happen.
https://www.thewaywardhome.com/make-money-living-on-the-road/
http://www.alwaystheroad.com/blog/2017/9/18/the-ultimate-van-life-

question-answered-how-we-make-money-on-the-road
https://projectvanlife.com/van-life-money-tips/
https://vansage.com/remote-jobs-for-van-life/
https://outboundliving.com/working-making-money/
https://vacayvans.com/how-to-make-money-working-remotely-living-vanlife/
https://wandrlymagazine.com/article/make-money-in-a-van/

On the Topic of Food

Everyone has different tastes, so we tried to round up a bunch of links that cover food storage, food preparation, and on-the-road recipes that many people can relate to. The food suggestions we mentioned within the chapter aren't inclusive of all diets and preferences, so we wanted to help get the creative cooking ideas flowing with a handful of resources.

https://www.climbonmaps.com/cold-food-storage.html
https://authenticavl.com/van-life/how-to-keep-your-food-fresh/
https://vanclan.co/vanlife-recipes/
https://mpora.com/camping/12-super-simple-meals-for-when-youre-living-in-a-van/
https://www.vancognito.com/van-life-cooking/
https://www.allrecipes.com/article/three-ways-to-conquer-camper-van-cooking-vanlife/
https://vansage.com/easy-campsite-recipes/
https://theplaidzebra.com/these-5-cheap-and-easy-meal-ideas-will-give-you-the-freedom-to-take-life-on-the-road/
https://simplyvanlife.com/non-perishable-foods-for-van-life/
https://www.parkedinparadise.com/storage-organization/
http://www.nomadswithavan.com/van-friendly-foods/
https://www.youtube.com/watch?v=1zTzaeOo8_w

LITTLE HOME BIG DREAMS

The Tiny Home Lifestyle For Beginners

INTRODUCTION

There's nothing wrong with taking up a lot of space. After all, every type of animal has its territory and builds a habitat best suited to its needs.

For some, that's a cozy, warm nest in which to raise our young.
For others, it's an aesthetic network of rooms and halls.
Others still prefer a tiny cocoon to protect and nurture them.

Just as every unique critter has developed its own tastes in homes and habitats, so, too, have humans created a diverse palette of possibilities. Some require palatial mansions or at least one bedroom for each person in the house.

But there's a new trend among modern housing, one that provides a broad sense of flexibility with a strict sense of minimalism. Though those terms sound almost completely polar opposite, there is one housing style that is equal parts wide open spaces and no frills: that of the Tiny Home.

The tiny home lifestyle has a lot of appeal. Much as a cocoon is associated with a certain protective coziness, the tiny home is a shell that provides just enough space to sustain human survival. Every part of the tiny home is strategically planned to be useful, with no corners cut and not a single millimeter unaccounted for.

Many of us are drawn to the idea of having no more space than we need. We're sick and tired of mowing lawns and manicuring the shrubbery. Very few people get a huge kick out of cleaning streaks off room after room of window glass, and keeping the floors clean is a fool's errand.

Add on top of that the giant house payments that come with even a reasonably-sized home, taxes, utilities, insurance ... the list of the financial responsibilities of homeownership seems almost endless.

Apartment and condo dwelling also has its shortcomings. The borrowed space may never quite feel right. In many cases, you lack the ability to make it a true "home," with clauses in your homeowner's association covenants, condo board mandates, or apartment lease preventing remodeling and even painting.

Tiny home living, for many, is the perfect intersection of having a space of your own without having a ridiculously large physical and financial responsibility. We're speaking, of course, in terms of actual size. While the common understanding is that tiny houses come with a tiny price tag, we'll soon discover that isn't always the case. But when it comes to having a potentially portable, bespoke dwelling that fits your every movement, a tiny home is ideal for many people.

Transitioning from a standard-sized two- or three-bedroom house to a tiny house may seem like it wouldn't be a very big jump, but there are many factors that need to be considered before leaving your current home behind.

For many people reading this book, tiny home living is something on the horizon. Depending on the research and exploration you've done so far, that horizon might be years in the future, or you might be ready to write your first check as soon as you put this book down. Regardless of where you are in the decision-making process, you likely have many questions.

There are a lot of steps in the process of finding the perfect tiny house for your lifestyle. But first, you need to make sure that transitioning to a tiny home lifestyle is the right fit for you. In this book, we'll explore the pros and cons of the tiny life. You'll want to be prepared for every challenge and reward that you meet along the way.

Next, you'll need to know how to get started. It turns out that the road to a tiny house is filled with twists and turns and sometimes even trailers. You'll want to be armed with a significant amount of information before you take the plunge on tiny house dwelling.

There are many things you'll want to keep in mind along the journey as well. We'll take you on a room-by-room, or rather pod-by-pod, tour of your prospective tiny house to explore the different things you'll want to factor in, whether you're buying a prefabricated or custom tiny home or building it yourself.

From mortgages to mobility, there are plenty of details you'll need to keep in mind when preparing to leave your house, apartment, or condominium behind for the tiny life. This book is intended to keep those concepts organized so that you have the smoothest move possible. While there will surely be a few bumps and bent nails along the way, you'll be armed with all the information you need to say goodbye to the things you like the least about your current living situation.

Within the pages of this book, you'll find details as to what constitutes a "tiny house," and what you need to keep in mind when it comes to financing, building, and finding the perfect location for your new dwelling. Though the concept of living in tiny homes is growing rapidly in popularity, there are many considerations that haven't quite caught up to the notion, such as insurance coverage, mortgage options, and even finding an appropriate spot to call home. These waters can prove difficult to navigate for the uninitiated, so we'll be sure to walk through each potential challenge in detail.

We'll also focus considerably on the tiny home lifestyle. You may already realize that your giant dining room table isn't going to have a place in your new habitat, but that begs the question: Where are you going to eat instead? What about watching TV or reading a book? You'll need to plan out a space that reflects your lifestyle and provides ample opportunity for you to go about your regular day. This includes tips for minimizing, maximizing, and even making your home feel cozy and personal, regardless of the lack of space.

Lastly, we'll get ready for long-term tiny house living, covering topics such as cleaning, composting, and how to add kids and pets to the fold. Though you may not be able to imagine the possibilities now, we'll share some very helpful tips and tricks that can reduce chaos while amplifying your comfort level in your new home.

This book is written from the perspective of homeowners in the United States, but the concept of making the most out of very little room is universal. With the exception of land, towing, insurance, and financial considerations, the information found in this book can be helpful for anyone looking to maximize their miniature space.

At the end of this book, you'll find a Resources section with links and references to various sources that can help inspire and guide you along the way. You'll also find outlets to the tiny home community. As it so happens, tiny home dwellers have many groups, forums, and sites across the internet where they share new ideas and advice as well as collaborate on new concepts. This community can be invaluable for new members looking for tips, tricks, and a sympathetic ear.

As you read on, you may find yourself wanting to make notes, so feel free to keep a notebook or tablet handy. I very much recommend this method, as you'll find yourself wanting to remember certain ideas and concepts. You'll also be doing a lot of research along the way, so you may want to keep all of your thoughts organized in one centralized area. I refer to "your notebook or journal" several times throughout the text, but I appreciate that most people have "gone digital," so this can mean whatever note-taking, thought-remembering, and dream-capturing method you've established to keep you organized through this process.

You may also be inspired to create a vision board to store some key inspirational notes on a site such as Pinterest. Feel free to do so, as being prepared and aware is one of the best ways to become successful in your transition to tiny home living. The goal of this book is to leave you feeling confident and comfortable in your decision—whether you immediately proceed with your tiny house plans or not.

There is no wrong way to live in a tiny house, just as there's no wrong way to live in a home of any size or configuration. Still, many people who have made the move themselves recommend a certain level of preparation and research before getting too invested in the process. Read on to learn if tiny living is right for you, and how to get ready for the lifestyle changes associated with the switch!

AUTHOR'S NOTE: HOW WE FELL INTO TINY HOUSE LIVING

My own tiny house journey was entirely unplanned and completely unexpected.

If you have read any of my previous books, you'll know that my husband Brad and I have been happily living the van life since 2018. I decided to walk away from corporate America to pursue my dream of being a freelance writer. Brad had been working remotely with the same company for several years. We employed a lot of creativity, made a whole bunch of mistakes, and set out to explore the country in our 1985 Volkswagen Vanagon.

Then came 2020. The year started out pretty normally. We were starting the year by circulating among our friends and families, crashing in their spare rooms or driveways so we could catch up and ride out that holiday spirit as long as possible. Plus, it gave us the chance to drive as little as possible while the weather was still being dicey.

When the COVID-19 pandemic was announced, Brad and I weren't sure quite how to handle it. Living in a van was fine, and relatively low risk, but how were we going to handle the everyday stuff? Grocery stores were running out of food and supplies, campgrounds were shutting down, and city-wide curfews were being enacted across the country. A sense of dread, bordering on panic, set in.

We didn't want to rent an apartment because that would require a lease. Plus, some places weren't even showing or renting to new tenants due to lockdown restrictions. It felt like we were stranded at the end of the Earth with no opportunities to settle down. Think **Mad Max,** only with a lot of stops at gas stations and flavored water.

We considered buying an investment property, then renting it out when we got back on the road again, but that seemed like way too much work. We'd already sold our houses before, and neither of us had the motivation to do any remodeling. We had no furniture, limited supplies, and extremely limited time. Since Brad works in absence management, he was glued to his phone and laptop twelve to fourteen hours every day.

The solution came out of nowhere. One of Brad's work contacts owns a farm in the middle of Illinois. On this farm is a cabin he had recently rehabbed. His idea was to turn it into a vacation rental, but COVID-19 had shut that plan down very quickly. Instead, he asked us if we'd like to rent it until it was practical to get back on the road again.

Initially, I thought the transition from van to tiny house was no big deal. In fact, the extra room seemed downright luxurious. I could sit upright in bed without whacking my head on the ceiling. Brad could be upstairs, and I could be downstairs—we could be separated by an entire layer of space! We finally had running water and electricity and climate control. For the first time in years, I wasn't haunted by sand and gravel that had been tracked into the tiniest corners of the van.

But there are aspects of the lifestyle that are very different from living in a regular-sized house or even a van. Our home is on a fixed foundation, so our travel possibilities are limited. We've even purchased an inexpensive car so we don't have to run errands in the van. Our shower is in a detached building, which we fondly call "the indoor outhouse." The view—which is extraordinarily gorgeous—doesn't change from day-to-day. We have indoor cooking options, but we still like to use the fire pit and grill as often as possible. What I'm saying is that tiny house living will always be exactly what *you* make it. Furthermore, you shouldn't try to force your lifestyle into a tiny house or vice versa. There are so many options and possibilities today that you don't have to scramble and buy the first tiny house you see, even if you're a van-lifer looking for a port during a pandemic.

Thankfully, Brad's buddy gave us a lot of leeway with the cabin. We were able to outfit it in a way that makes sense to us. At the same time, this has given me a lot of time to think about all the things I might do differently if I were to do it again. We've done quite a bit of research into adapting our lifestyle from the van to a THOW (a tiny house on wheels), and it's very appealing to us. That being said, we are going to take our time before we take any next steps and really evaluate where we're going and what we're doing.

This book came out of a place of opportunities and possibilities. I was surrounded by so much research that it seemed inevitable that I would write a book about our journey and share tips and tricks I wish I had considered … or even thought to consider … when we were arranging our transition. As you read on, I encourage you to really take the time to consider what you want and what you need. I repeat that a lot, but truly, think of this as an opportunity to make your dreams come true.

CHAPTER 1: GETTING STARTED

First things first: Before you start giving away your belongings and packing the necessities, let's look at what a tiny house really is. Sure, the pictures online look great, and everyone seems to be smiling and having a good time. But how did they get to this point?

Moving into a tiny home isn't going to solve all of your problems instantly. In fact, living in a new environment is going to provide you with a whole new set of challenges. There are obstacles intrinsic to any type of lifestyle, but in order to find success in a new lifestyle, you have to be aware of these challenges as well as willing and able to meet them head on.

In this chapter, we'll take a look at what a tiny house really is. That doesn't just mean the textbook definition of a "tiny house" but a glimpse into the associated daily trials and tribulations of living in such a space. This book is intended to guide readers through understanding and appreciating the tiny house lifestyle, but I feel it's important to set the scene. There are so many things that are advertised or described as a "tiny lifestyle," so how do you figure out what aspects of that lifestyle you like, don't like, or don't even understand yet?

You're likely familiar with the concept of a "tiny house." After all, the name is pretty self-explanatory. But what defines a tiny house, as opposed to just a really small house? What are the advantages of a tiny house over a small house? Does it differ from mobile home or RV living? Let's take a look at the very basics to answer these questions and to help you get started on your own tiny home journey.

Section 1: What is a Tiny Home?

This is actually a loaded question. There are many factors which go into determining what is and isn't a tiny house as you're soon to discover. You can find a variety of options branded as "tiny houses" online, from 800 square foot cottages, to 600 square foot mobile homes, to portable shacks that seem barely habitable for the long-term resident.

According to the 2018 version of the International Residential Code, Appendix Q:

> *"A Tiny House is considered a Dwelling that is 400 square feet in floor area or less, excluding lofts . . . A Dwelling Unit is a single unit that provides complete independent living facilities such as living, sleeping, eating, cooking and sanitation."*

The code goes on to define all of the structural requirements for a tiny home, including ceilings:

1. *Habitable spaces and Hallways shall not have a ceiling height less than 6 feet 8 inches.*
2. *Bathrooms, Toilet rooms, and Kitchens shall not have a ceiling height less than 6 feet 4 inches.*
3. *Lofts are permitted to be less than 6 feet 8 inches. No minimum stated.*

Since the lofts are not part of the dwelling floor area, the rules for it are separate:

> *Lofts shall have a minimum floor area not less than 35 square feet.*
> *Lofts shall not be less than 5 feet in any horizontal dimension.*

However, in this case, floor area is not measured in areas where a roof slopes closer than 3 feet from the floor, so a sharply sloping roof can impact this measurement.

While something called the "International Residential Code" may seem like a pretty final authority on building codes, the truth is that codes can vary from location to location. Each city, county, or town can have their own set of rules and regulations for what people can and can't consider a tiny house in their area. In fact, this is possibly the most challenging part of owning a tiny home as you'll see when we discuss topics such as mortgages and insurance.

Additionally, while construction inside the tiny houses is generally less regulated than its footprint, this may be something to start researching now in the pre-planning stages. In the Resources section, you'll find a few links to sites that can get you started finding and understanding the requirements and restrictions in your area.

Remember, too, that these regulations apply to permanent structures on foundations. If you've decided you'd like to live in a THOW (Tiny House on Wheels) you'll not only need to look at structural guidelines but also trailering regulations, the legal requirements for on-road travel, and parking stipulations as well.

Therefore, it's important to start looking and learning right out of the gate before you make any sort of final purchase or decision. Is the home of your dreams considered a tiny home in the place where you'd like to put it? In some cases, you might find that your ideal dwelling is considered a small house.

Does that mean you should put down this book immediately and go back to the drawing board? Absolutely not! Living in a tiny house is all about the lifestyle, and while one municipality might state that you live in a small house, it is still very much your home to enjoy as you please. As you continue to read and research, you'll find that there are plenty of technicalities that will dampen your spirit if you let them. If tiny house living is truly your dream, then rally on! There are plenty of homeowners around the world who have also overcome these challenges to pursue their ideal lifestyle.

Aside from building codes and regulations, the size of your tiny home will be based on your own preferences. According to many tiny home dwellers, there is definitely a learning curve when moving into your new space full-time. They report that one very important consideration is purchasing or constructing a home space that fits your general daily flow. For example, if going up and down a ladder is difficult for you, then a home with a loft bed might not be ideal.

Another fun feature of tiny homes is their unique exteriors. You can find nods to all sorts of architectural styles: from itty-bitty Tudor-style homes with stucco exteriors, to miniature Swiss chalets with high pitched roofs, to log cabins or Antebellum-style abodes that have signature pillars on the porch. There seems to be a notion among those less familiar with the tiny house movement that these are little more than shacks or sheds. Spacewise, it would be difficult to argue against this sentiment. But as far as creating warm, welcoming, functional living spaces, tiny houses are far removed from your regular backyard shed.

As you longingly cruise through online pictures of tiny homes and miniature houses, you may notice that it seems like no two are the same. Many people choose to design and construct their own tiny house from the ground up.

One huge benefit to this is that you will be able to create a space that fits your ideal lifestyle. We'll dive further into the pros and cons of prefabricated homes versus building your own in the next chapter, but for now, keep in mind that you may have more control over the flow of your future home than you might with a three-bedroom house in a suburban neighborhood.

While many of these homes are fully mobile, some are planted on permanent foundations. Once again, codes and regulations are in charge here. There are some locations in which putting a building less than a certain square footage on a lot may not be considered a homestead, regardless of the fact that you have no intention of moving it. There are also locations wherein you can freely construct whatever you feel like building, so don't be discouraged until you've fully explored scenarios in your preferred location.

At the same time, many tiny house dwellers appreciate the mobile option. Many homes have been designed with the idea of being able to load them onto a flatbed trailer and transporting them from location to location based on the seasons or even the owner's whims. The possibility of relocating at any time is often a huge draw to those who appreciate a less rigid and structured lifestyle but still enjoy four solid walls and a roof.

"Versatility" is a word thrown around often in the tiny home community. It refers not only to the structure itself, which can be hauled from place to place with surprisingly little effort, but the interior as well. Without multiple rooms for various purposes—such as a bathroom, bedroom, and kitchen—each space must be versatile. As you leaf through the examples on Instagram or Pinterest, you'll notice an eating area can double as a desk, or a seating arrangement unfolds to become a bed. There's a certain amount of flexibility that comes with tiny living.

That flexibility needs to be reflected in each individual owner as well. This is not to say that you need to be able to do a backbend to get into the bathroom but that you are not the type of person who requires large spaces for languishing. You need to be okay with being able to touch every wall with your arms outstretched, depending on your interior design. Therefore, before you get started, it's important to understand why tiny living is a thing, and whether you're on board with the overall goals and results that can be found in such a unique way of living.

Another thing to keep in mind as you proceed through this exercise is whether you really want a tiny home or just a small space. Micro apartments and condos do exist and might be an option to consider before you go all-in on a tiny house. There are pros and cons to these dwellings of course. You won't have the freedoms available from owning your space, and taking your house on the road with you is definitely out of the question. You'll have to share walls with neighbors, and in some cases, smaller apartments have bigger issues.

The exercises in the following sections will help you appreciate the "whys" of your desire to live in a tiny home and, hopefully, extract some of the deeper thoughts and feelings related to the topic. While we may be tempted to just do it, the topic of homeownership and planning for the rest of your life deserves a little deliberation. Read on to discover the pros and cons of tiny home living, and consider how these changes will impact your lifestyle.

Section 2: The goals of living in a tiny home

There are many positive rewards for living in a tiny home, most of which can be classified under the umbrella term "saving." Those who live in tiny houses will be saving space, saving money, and saving the environment in the long run. That being said, the advantages of living in a very small dwelling aren't always outright and abundant.

As you are defining your proposed tiny home lifestyle, always bring yourself back to the reason you want to do this in the first place. Why do you want to ditch the neighborhood and go tiny?

There are likely several reasons which extend beyond the pesky shrubbery and steam cleaning acres of carpets. While those are certainly big-time motivators for trying your hand at minimalism, there are multiple solutions for those issues that aren't quite so life-altering or permanent.

Therefore, as you loudly object that you really **do** want less space, ask yourself again, "Why?" What about your life would change dramatically if you were to leave your current abode and live in what many people proclaim to be "a glorified shack?"

The romantic and aesthetic appeal are often towards the top of the list when it comes to reasons people want to try tiny house living. The consolidated interiors look fantastic. If you're not wasting a single inch, then there aren't huge, ugly light fixtures, or awkward unused wall space. In a tiny home, everything truly has a purpose. The deliberate details that owners put into these homes can be a huge draw for those who have lived their entire lives in unimaginative houses or apartments.

There's a certain dollhouse element to the aesthetic as well. Tiny houses are twee and resourceful, with a "waste not, want not" outlook that combines function with looking cute. And owners decorating the outsides as very small castles, log cabins, or Swiss chalets proves that they are meant to look as cute as they come across.

The consolidated lifestyle echoes the simplicity that we all crave in life. Life is incredibly hectic for many of us. Eliminating as much stress as possible has become a survival technique; in a sense, we're all trying to save ourselves from any stressor that can be easily eliminated. Our superfluous stuff, the feathers that pad our nests, can be soothing and stressful, sometimes all at once.

Would you feel more comfortable in your home if you didn't have to walk past that awkward bare spot on the wall? Would you feel less anxious if you didn't have to keep your vast collection of knickknacks in tip-top shape?

We all have things that we collect, and many of us go into collection mode when we're very stressed out. There are loads of psychological concepts and motivations behind this behavior, such as wanting something positive to inspire hope in our lives or to have a physical reminder of the time and effort we have put into a certain task evidenced by that big splurge we often make after a particularly large work bonus or overtime check. But do we really need that stuff, or is the burden of caring for that stuff making our stress worse?

In a tiny home, it is virtually impossible to collect things, regardless of how subconsciously your brain may make purchases. You'll find yourself growing more and more creative as you divest your collections of this and that.

Think about putting all of your favorite geegaws in a single desk drawer. All of them. Can you do that? More importantly, do you want to do that? Nearly everyone is capable of narrowing down their collections, but when you attempt this exercise, how do you feel? Accomplished? Or maybe you feel a profound sense of loss. Either reaction is perfectly valid, but if you find yourself grieving your belongings, perhaps a different type of minimalism is in your future.

Echoing the teachings of Henry David Thoreau, withdrawing to nature with only the most basic of necessities can restore balance to your peace of mind … right? It turns out, there might be something to that "hippie-dippy nature stuff." If you choose to build a tiny home on a permanent foundation, you may find yourself getting creative with zoning laws and property lines. If you build a THOW, you'll be able to pick up and move on a whim. Being in control of your location at all times can be a very freeing experience, allowing you to retreat to your own version of Walden Pond and come back to civilization as you wish.

Of course, as mentioned earlier, there might be some legal red tape and hazy legality on that location front too. Still, you'll definitely use fewer utilities, even if you were to set up your tiny house in the backyard of your current home. It would be impossible for a tiny home to require as much energy and water as a full-sized house, so you're guaranteed smaller bills.

You can also go completely off-grid if you feel like it. Thanks to advances in generators, composting toilets, water tanks, and solar power, a tiny house can be rigged to be completely self-sustaining in a sense. You'll still need to empty the toilet and change out the greywater tanks, but your tiny home can be as efficient as any camper van or motorhome. If you choose a permanent location that's appropriately zoned for it, you can even grow a garden, collect rainwater, raise chickens … the sky's the limit!

But each time you find yourself getting excited about these prospects, dial back to asking yourself "Why?" You can start a garden nearly anywhere, thanks to container solutions and indoor grow stations. You can fit most homes with solar panels, and if you really felt like it, you could use little to no electricity at any time. So what is it about doing so in a tiny house that gets you more excited about these concepts?

For those who happily live in tiny homes, the winning combination is a little bit of all of these categories. Choosing your own location, off the grid, with minimal distractions, and living in a fully self-supported manner sounds like a challenge to lots of folks, but many see this challenge as a dream come true.

Section 3: Challenges of living in a tiny home

So what are the downsides to living in a tiny home? Sure, it sounds like the local and legal stuff can be a bit of a hassle, but in a perfect world, what could possibly be bad about living in a tiny house?

It turns out that just because a space is small doesn't mean it requires less upkeep. True, it will not take you very long to sweep a house the size of your current bedroom. That being said, you may find yourself sweeping every single day or even multiple times a day.

Just because your home is tiny doesn't mean the dirt somehow shrinks too. If you wear muddy boots into your tiny home, your dirty footprints will need to be cleaned up right away, lest the dirt should track further and further into your home. Parents of very small children are familiar with this phenomenon, but for the uninitiated, every tiny little mess will magically spread before your very eyes. You'll notice dust more easily too. Not only will you be able to see it with your eyes, but if you have allergies, you'll definitely feel the effects.

One thing that many people aren't prepared for when they make the switch to tiny houses is the frequency of cleaning. In a standard-sized home, you can do things like leave an empty glass on the coffee table overnight or save doing the dinner dishes until morning. Granted, the people who raised you might have a thing or two to say about such habits, but let's face it, none of us are perfect housekeepers.

In a tiny house, however, you're almost forced to be a near-perfect housekeeper. One rule of thumb of leaving things out is that it's going to stink or get in the way. That cup of cold coffee sitting in your sink will not only make the entire house smell like coffee due to the small confines of space, but it's most likely going to take up your entire sink space.

Furthermore, certain cleaning activities are going to be a lot different in a tiny house. Next time you make the bed in your current bedroom, ask yourself how your process would change if the bed took up the entire room. Where would you store your clean sheets? How would you wash your sheets? What kind of weird yoga positions will you need to practice to both strip your bed of the dirty sheets and put clean ones on? There are actually videos (linked in the Resources section at the end of this book) of tiny house residents demonstrating tasks such as these, which folks who live in standard-sized houses take for granted.

Let's go back to the coffee cup example. So your dirty coffee cup is in the sink, and you've decided you want a nice cup of tea. You reach for another cup, perhaps a clean cup in your cabinets ... but wait! This is a tiny house. You don't have loads of kitchen cupboards filled with cookware and cutlery. Living with very little space means that just a few items will fill that space. That's not to say that you have to use itty-bitty teacups and teeny-tiny plates, but if you choose to have a twenty-piece dinnerware set, you will need to sacrifice other just-as-necessary items to make the space for it.

Minimalism is key when it comes to tiny house living. You'll need to become very keen on things that can be used for multiple purposes and finding ingenious storage spots for things that aren't being currently used. Later in this book, we'll look at methods for minimizing your belongings without going completely bare, as well as explore some ideas for making the most of your space. For now, look around your house and get a feel for how much stuff you wouldn't mind getting rid of. Is this exercise challenging, or are you pretty okay with the idea of having a giant garage sale or donation party?

Another thing to consider is company. Do you like to have your friends over for dinner parties? Are you the type who likes to lounge out on the sofa with your buddies for movie night? Depending on the layout of your new home, that may or may not be difficult, but there are other things to consider about hanging out with your friends in your tiny home: Bathroom use, for example. Additionally, it might be tough to find places to hang all the coats and stash all of their shoes, depending on the weather. And if your kitchen is limited in cups and cutlery, will you ask them to bring their own if they come over for dinner?

When you're first considering tiny home living, these challenges might not seem like a big deal. It's all part of the experience, right? Absolutely. But before you get super-invested in planning for your small home switcheroo, really think about your lifestyle. What are some things you're willing to sacrifice? More importantly, what are some things you're definitely *not* interested in changing?

There are solutions to all of these challenges of course. With a little foresight and planning, you'll be able to troubleshoot and accommodate. Just like any major lifestyle change, things will feel awkward and maybe a little uncomfortable at first, but you'll come to find your stride over time and continue to learn and grow into your tiny home.

However, if any of these challenges seem like it may be too uncomfortable, this is a good time to explore that situation more. You might feel that your concerns are ridiculous, but it's far better to address a ridiculous concern now than to invest all of your time and money into a tiny house you'll ultimately not enjoy.

One common exercise to help you understand whether or not you'll like tiny house living is to mimic the scenario. There are a few different ways to do this:

1. Live in your bedroom for a week. For the purpose of this exercise, it's ok to use your bathroom as you normally would but try not to leave for any other reason. Cook all of your meals in your room, do all of your daily tasks in your room, and limit yourself to the items you have in your room. This means you'll have to plan ahead and pack everything you think you'll need for the week in your bedroom. This isn't going to be exactly identical to the tiny house experience, but you'll get a feel for your wants and needs in a small space, which is a great place to start on your tiny house journey.
2. Rent a small RV or camper van for a week. Again, not exactly the same, but there are several things you'll learn from this experience. First, you'll gain an appreciation for living in a space in which every square inch is designed to be fully functional or even multi-purpose. You'll get insight into how much space is available for storage and

movement as well as ideas on how to maximize your minimal belongings. You can also get accustomed to using a composting toilet and greywater system, which are very common among the tiny house community.

3. Try renting a rustic cabin or tiny home for the weekend. Some campgrounds or holiday resorts actually offer tiny home rentals on their grounds. This can be a risk-averse way to find out not only if you're comfortable with the lifestyle but can also give you some ideas about changes you'd make to the layout or flow in your own tiny house.

If you choose to complete one of these exercises, you may wish to keep a journal to make notes about the experience. Notice what changes about your daily routine when your living space is diminished. Are you finding yourself wishing you had more space in a particular area? What are some things you didn't fully plan for? What are some surprises that came up along the way? Make notes about what you would change if this was your entire living area and reflect on the experience often.

At this stage of the game, you still have plenty of decisions to make. Even if you are 100 percent green-lighting the move to a tiny house, your best move at this point is to start the research and weigh your options. While most of us hate the anxiety and anticipation of a long, drawn-out process, this is one area in which having patience and doing the legwork before you make a huge investment can pay off big time.

If you're like many people preparing for a major lifestyle shift, you're probably near-obsessively cruising sales sites, social media, and watching all the television shows you can regarding tiny homes in order to prepare. This is definitely a good idea, as the more exposure you get to the concept, the more ideas and knowledge you'll have as you creep closer and closer towards your own dream home. But remember: a lot of what you see on television has been scripted and edited for entertainment value. Social media posts are filtered to look good for the viewer. What you're seeing is a fully scrubbed, filtered, and viewer-friendly peek into a much more complex reality.

We're not saying to avoid these outlets of expression; on the contrary, it's a great opportunity to see a variety of different styles, options, and choices made by others who have traveled a similar path. But if you're going to embrace a tiny house lifestyle, that means taking it all in. In addition to researching fun things, like storage solutions, look at less-exciting necessities, like toilets and greywater systems. In addition to looking at pictures on Instagram, follow some frank and honest blogs too. A few options have been included in the Resources section to help you get started on this search.

In the next chapter, we'll look at what it takes to find exactly the right tiny home, including the pros and cons of various construction options. While it may be incredibly tempting to pull the trigger on the first functioning tiny house you see, remember that this is more of a process than simply moving your belongings from one place to another.

Many people like to keep a journal or notebook during a huge life change like this to keep track of their thoughts and ideas. This is a fantastic idea, especially if you're trying to juggle your regular lifestyle on top of making changes. If you choose to do so, here are some topics to really consider at this stage of your tiny home journey:

- Why do I want to live in a tiny home?
- What do I need to take with me?
- Where do I want to put my tiny home?
- What are some things I love about the tiny house lifestyle?
- What will be more difficult about my lifestyle in a tiny house?

As you read through the next chapter, you can also use this journal to make notes about tiny houses you like, features that you love, and surprises that you find along the way. You want to make as many notes as you can at this point, because as your new lifestyle takes shape, you'll want to revisit your thoughts and opinions. Don't be surprised if they change frequently too. The more you learn about tiny house living, the more you'll appreciate taking the time to get organized now.

CHAPTER 2: FINDING A TINY HOME

Finding your very own tiny home and locating a place to put it are equally important, which is why we've devoted a full chapter to each topic. It's a little bit of a "chicken and the egg" scenario. As stated earlier, there are plenty of laws and regulations which dictate the minimum square footage of a permanent home which can prevent you from simply buying a lot in any old neighborhood and throwing up your tiny home.

At the same time, knowing what type of tiny home you want is going to help you narrow down where you can put it. For example, if you decide you want an A-frame on a foundation, you'll be able to specifically research locations where that's permissible and go from there in choosing your exact plot of land, finding a lender, builder, insurance, and so on.

Some folks may find that purchasing a tiny house before you have a plan for locating it is very much putting the cart before the horse, and we couldn't agree more. The purpose of this chapter isn't to encourage you to rush out and make a purchase as soon as you're done with the last section but instead to help make you aware of the options that are out there. There are prefabricated tiny homes, build-your-own kits that can be customized, shipping containers or school bus conversions, and there's even the option to just go for it and design and construct your own home from the nails to the shingles.

Therefore, the purpose of this chapter is to provide a practical introduction to all of these options so that you can personally weigh the pros and cons of each before you take the plunge. You'll be able to decide what you want, what you can live with, and what you definitely want to avoid before you put down that first payment. From here, we'll guide you through choosing a location and looking at the legal aspects, but first, let's take a look at some of the most common types of tiny houses to get you started on your research.

Section 1: Prefabricated tiny houses

"Prefabricated" or "prefab" is used to describe houses that have already been constructed. These houses already exist and can be purchased "as is."

When it comes to tiny houses, there are actually a few different versions of this. For example, there are actual tiny houses that have been built over the years and exist as permanent structures in towns and cities around the world. We tend to think of this type of structure as a recent phenomenon, but you'll find very small cottages and 600-square foot and under homes dating back to the early days when your area was settled. After all, the first structures of any civilization weren't elaborate three-bedroom split-levels with basements and central air!

If you're interested in a historic tiny house, you'll need to do a little research. That means searching through real estate listings until you find something that meets your needs and dreams. They aren't impossible to find, but they may be located in out-of-the-way areas. If that's part of the draw of tiny homes for you, then you're definitely on the right track.

To start looking for an already-existing, permanent-on-a-foundation, someone-has-already-lived-there tiny house like this, head to the online real estate sites. Many of them provide search criteria such as square footage and location, so you can get a feel for what options might be available. You may not find exactly what you're looking for, but you will be able to get a feel for the market in a particular location.

You'll also have the option to shop new and pre-owned tiny houses on wheels. A good place to shop for these is online forums for tiny house enthusiasts. We've included a few links to some websites that can point you in the right direction in the Resources section at the end of this book.

There are many pros and cons to choosing a prefabricated or pre-owned tiny home. Most importantly, bear in mind that your house will already be completely constructed. If you're shopping for your first tiny house, and you're not particularly handy or well-versed in structural codes and the construction process, this might be a great starting place for you, since everything has been laid out in careful consideration for codes and creating an ideal living space for many homeowners.

However, this also means you will have very little opportunity to modify or customize your new house. A smaller footprint means that everything is purposefully built in its place for a reason, so attempting to update one feature, such as counter space in the kitchen, may require an entire remodel of the entire building.

On the other hand, some people purchase a prefab structure without interior walls for the purpose of doing a complete remodel of the inside space. Many of the code regulations that apply to tiny houses specifically mention the exterior of the dwelling, so having an exterior that adheres to local regulations can help you get your foot in the door of a tiny home (pun intended).

So while a prefab tiny house can be updated, it may be a lengthy, strenuous process. It will require expert understanding of construction and engineering, as well as tools, lumber, and other supplies. You'll need to have a place to live while you're doing the renovation, since the small space more or less precludes being able to live under the roof while you're making updates.

Then there's the overall cost. Already built houses will always cost more than a load of lumber and a building permit. Since you're buying an existing structure, you'll want to be aware of the price per square foot as well as any relevant taxes. You may want to shop around a location to make sure that the price is fair and that you're not being taken for a ride due to the oddity of the commodity. Still, if you're purchasing an already standing home, it may be easier for you to secure a mortgage and insurance, especially if it's on a foundation and has been for quite some time.

Section 2: Building your own tiny home

The second option is to build your own tiny home. Much like purchasing a prefab house, there are different ways to accomplish this goal. The choice you make depends on how hands-on and do-it-yourself you are willing to be as well as how much time you have to dedicate to the process.

Remember, once you get started, you're going to have to follow this project to the end. That means you'll need to have a dedicated timeline for construction and completion. This timeline can vary greatly, depending on your budget and level of expertise. You'll want to ensure you have a place to live while you complete construction and plenty of time budgeted for mishaps and other calamity.

Time spent and money spent often go hand in hand when it comes to budgeting for a tiny house build. If you're building the entire dwelling on your own, you'll need to pay for every bent nail and stripped screw that goes into the process, and that can add up to lots of dollars and lost time if you're not extremely confident and competent in your construction skills.

However, there are a few options which can assist on this front. Many hardware or lumber outlets have created tiny house kits. Some of these simply include detailed plans and instructions for your build, while others actually include pre-cut lumber and fittings.

Naturally, these kits range in price, depending on the complexity of the build and the contents. They are very convenient, and in many cases, already rated to code—meaning they already meet the guidelines for housing. Much like with the prefab houses, you might lose a bit of customization, but you'll know you're getting a safe, livable house with all of the storage and function details already thought out for you.

You can also create your own plans and build your tiny home from scratch. If you choose this path, research is extremely important. Many things work very well on paper yet somehow don't translate well to reality. We've all seen construction fails with doors that don't open correctly, stairs that lead to walls, and toilets that are close enough to the front door that anyone can peek in. Before you create your own miniature Winchester Mystery House, make sure you really pay attention to all of your measurements.

You'll also need to be super diligent about construction codes in your location. Building a tiny house only to not be able to live in it would be truly tragic though an important and expensive life lesson. Rather than face the heartache of having a useless structure on your hands, self-builders will need to be fully informed. In fact, it may be helpful to hire a contractor or engineer experienced in tiny house building to help you navigate the process.

Another interesting option you have when constructing your own tiny home is a choice in materials. Our tiny home is constructed out of reclaimed materials. The lower floor was a one-room log cabin constructed in 1865. The builder tried very hard to salvage as much of the original structure as possible, but whatever couldn't be reused in the construction of the current tiny house went towards another project, and he substituted decommissioned telephone poles in their place. Even the cabinets are constructed from a barn that previously stood on his property.

When you choose to build your own tiny house, you definitely have greater control over the plans, the utilities, the appliances … essentially every aspect will be hand-picked for your needs. In the case of our current home, this allowed the builder to reuse perfectly good parts and pieces for a very green, very cost-efficient tiny home construction process.

He confirmed that this required a lot of effort though. Not only did he have to find all the right pieces of lumber, but he had to find someone who was willing to do the cutting, since he lacked the space and equipment to turn telephone poles into planks.

Since you aren't just making a major run to a hardware store, you may also find your project stalling while you refurbish a particular piece. Alternatively, you can search for the perfect salvage item to finish your current area of building.

So if you're not the most patient person, or you have a timeline by which you need to have your tiny house in livable condition, using strictly salvage items may not be the best option for you. Remember, there is no right and wrong, as long as you're meeting the local building codes and requirements. If the roof stays on in rough weather, and the doors open and close correctly, then you've got the hardest parts of the process under control. But if it really is important to you to use salvage materials and green, sustainable construction processes, then bear in mind that you might have to extend your timeline and prepare for delays.

Lastly, you'll need a place to build it. Unlike a bookshelf or coffee table, this isn't a project that will fit in your garage or rec room. Sure, certain parts can be constructed independently from the full structure, but at some point, you will have a fully-constructed tiny home shell that's ready for drywall, plumbing, and electricity. Where are you going to put all of these parts, and more importantly, where are you going to put them all together?

Much like renovating a van or RV, building a THOW will require room for the "wheels and up." That means you'll either construct your home on top of the trailer and build from the wheels up, or you'll construct your home first, then lift it and secure it to the trailer. Either way, you'll need to have a space that has clearance enough to fit an entire house. The other dimensions are also important, but height is an added component that truly needs to be considered. Building a tiny home that won't be able to leave the garage can be a very complicated problem!

As far as the location itself, you'll want a spot that has access to power or a reliable generator so you can use your tools and spotlights as needed. You'll also need plenty of space for construction as well as the ability to store and lock up things like small fixtures, tools, and metal, lest they wander off in the middle of the night. Some localities have very strict rules about putting up another structure on the same lot as a house, regardless of how temporary the setting may be, so before you throw up a tiny house in your backyard, find out if that's legal in your area.

Once you have a location set for construction, make sure you check out the noise ordinances. Your after-work build may be shut down after sunset, depending on where you live.

All in all, there are a lot of factors that go into determining whether a self build or kit-born tiny house is right for you. Making the ultimate, perfect-for-you, absolutely custom tiny house of your dreams with your own two hands is a beautiful goal and one many people hope to accomplish. However, it may not be the right time, place, or solution given your budget, your needs, and your deadlines.

Always weigh all of the facts along with the pros and cons of constructing your own tiny home. There are many emotional components to the process, but always be aware of the legal, practical, and financial aspects of your decision before you become too invested in your project.

Section 3: Deciding which version is best for you

As you can see, the path to living in a tiny house is lined with choices and decisions. At this point, your brain may be swarming with details and facts, things you like and don't like, and option after option that you find on the internet.

The system of organization you've developed is going to come in particularly handy for keeping all of these swirling thoughts in line. It's time to pull out the journal or notebook to get these thoughts jotted down before they spiral out of control or start swarming around noisily.

You've already examined why you want to live in a tiny house. You've taken the time to consider what features about this lifestyle appeal to you and some of the areas where you know you might have a harder time adjusting. You may feel that this list is no longer important, once you've green-lit your decision to move into a tiny home, but it's actually going to be very relevant to every choice you make going forward.

You see, everything that you have identified as a challenge when it comes to living in a very small dwelling can be manifested by the space you choose. As an example, let's say you indicated that you are intimidated or unsure of having a loft-style bedroom. You don't like the idea of crawling down a ladder if you have to go to the bathroom in the middle of the night, and you're absolutely certain you're going to crack your head on a pitched ceiling if you wake up suddenly. If you choose a space that has an elevated sleeping area and a steep roof, that challenge will continue to magnify itself every time you go to bed.

Alternately, let's say your soul-searching led you to discover that you aren't comfortable dealing with a composting toilet. Honestly, they're not that fun, and this is a completely reasonable discovery! In this case, maybe a THOW isn't the right idea for you, and you'd be much happier in a tiny historic home or apartment. The beautiful thing about all of these myriad choices and decisions is that, eventually, the pieces will align to create the perfect home for you.

Unless you are on a specific timeline, such as a job relocation, it's a good idea to take your time searching for a tiny house. In a regular-sized house, you can make accommodations for things you don't like without a giant disruption. In a prefabricated tiny house or tiny house kit, though, it's going to be much more difficult to repurpose or remodel an area, since all of the pieces and areas are specifically created to work as one.

At this stage, take the time to think about what you require from your tiny home. You've likely seen a lot of floor plans and layouts, so use those images to help you jot down a list of all of the things that you know you need and that you absolutely don't want. For example, some tiny houses have galley-style kitchens, while others have a flow-through lower level. Despite what some Instagram photos would tell you, not all tiny houses have a loft. Do you want a loft, or does that seem problematic for your particular lifestyle? Do you want an actual bathroom, or are you okay with an RV-style shower-with-a-toilet-in-it water closet?

If you discover that some of these things really aren't a priority to you, make note of that as well. Maybe you don't care if you have a porch or not. Perhaps windows aren't really something that concerns you because you plan to spend most of your time outside anyway. Conversely, you may want as many windows as possible because you don't want to use a generator for electric light. There truly are a ton of options to consider at this point.

This is your dream, so you're allowed to really think about what qualities you want your dream home to have. You may have to compromise on some of these things, but listing them out now and discovering what your priorities are will make the tiny house shopping process that much easier.

Once you've got your wants and needs identified, start shopping. Some people recommend starting shopping for exactly what you want. Personally, I find this to be a great way to become quickly discouraged and disappointed. When you're starting out, starry-eyed, dreaming big, things will look fantastic on paper only to not live up to expectations in person.

Therefore, I recommend looking at everything. At the very least, looking at something that you are pretty sure you don't want will help solidify your feelings that this is not the right choice for you. You may feel like looking at a tiny apartment is a dumb idea, because you definitely know you're leaving the city, but think of the space as a source of hands-on inspiration to help guide your list of what you definitely want in your very own space.

And, yes, that goes for those of you who are adamant about building your own tiny home as well. As mentioned earlier, there are kits and plans available, but you're still going to have your influence on this structure. You'll want to pay attention not only to the layout to ensure it works for your lifestyle, but by looking at existing models, you'll get a feel for a variety of floor plans and layouts and experience a lot of different innovative built-in and customization options.

Since innovation and customization are two of the tiny home tenets, these are definitely things to pay attention to. Things like cutting boards or desktops that slide in and out of countertops like a drawer help combat the lack of flat space in the kitchen, which can be a huge help if you like to take time to carefully prepare meals. Each time you look at a new tiny house, make notes in your journal about these features. Even if you have a visceral negative reaction to a space, it's still taught you something very important about your preferences and will guide your ultimate tiny house decision.

I recommend jotting down detailed notes before and after checking out each space, whether you do so in person or virtually. It doesn't have to be anything anyone else would even understand but enough information that when you revisit these notes later, you'll know exactly what you meant.

For example:

House #1

Square footage: 302

Built: 1865

Construction: FIXED FOUNDATION. Log cabin, rehabbed 1994 to add windows, tin roof, electric circuitry.

Price: $159,900

Notes: Open floor plan lower floor. Composting toilet/utility room under stairs. Sink in the kitchen area only. No interior shower (separate shed). Wood burning stove. Solar powered rain collection system. Solar panel electricity. Small furnace. Former fireplace updated into cold pantry with cupboard. Built-in bed upstairs.

House #2

Square footage: 225 + 89 in loft

Built: (custom, upon request)

Construction: THOW, Tumbleweed "ROANOKE 26' Alta"

Price: Starts at $78,000

Notes: Fully mobile. Queen sleeping area in loft, and queen sleeping area in flex room. Closet in a great room and loft. Under-stair washer/dryer. Counter space and shelves in the bathroom. Overhead shelves in kitchen with optional oven/optional microwave, cooktop and hood included. Stairs to loft. Flex room could serve as an office or great room space.

House #3

Square footage: 396

Built: (custom, upon request)

Construction: THOW, Tiny Portable Cedar Cabins, "Townsend Cottage"

Price: Starts at $68,000

Notes: Two full bedrooms with a bath off of the central kitchen/dining/living area. Full kitchen oven/hood/sink/fridge. Few standard built-ins. Room for custom storage options. Ceiling fans. Lots of natural light. Very flexible kitchen/dining/living area. Could repurpose the second bedroom as storage/office.

House #4

Square footage: 203 (150 sq. ft. main, 53 sq.ft. loft)

Built: PLANS ONLY

Construction: Kit, built on steel trailer, 84 Lumber, "Countryside"

Price: $500. (Includes list of materials, framing, sheathing, and cladding diagrams, floor plans, interior & exterior elevations, overall sections, and structural sheets. Emailed upon purchase.)

Notes: Built-ins include under-bench storage, desk/table surface, kitchen cabinets, exterior storage bins, full bathroom, storage under built-in ladder to loft, windows in loft for light/ventilation, cooktop/sink/mini-fridge in kitchen. Loft is large enough for a queen-sized mattress only.

This may feel like a lot of examples, but these are four actual real-life tiny houses. As you can see, the array of differences really is stunning. On top of that, the three that aren't pre-built can be completely customized with the finishes you prefer.

Looking at these four examples, which tiny house are you drawn to? What do you like about them? What do you find less appealing about each one?

There are no right or wrong answers to these questions, only features and options that are right and wrong for your lifestyle. The goal of a dream home is that you aren't faced with any nightmares when you actually live in it, so take this time to plan carefully and research everything.

If a kit house looks good to you, for example, drill down to learn more. What are the user reviews like for the kit? Is it easy to build? Has anyone noted any complications? Does it include helpful hints for construction? Has anyone had difficulty getting insurance based on these plans? Are there recommendations for appliances/electric/water/plumbing included, or are you expected to source that information separately?

What about a construction company? What types of experiences have others had with the company? Will they build anywhere or allow you to purchase the building specifications? Can you pick up your THOW once it's built or have it delivered? How will you check on progress? What type of trailer is required? Where are they based? For example, a company based in New Mexico may have different priorities for building than a company based in Minnesota based on the typical weather for each location.

The questions for each type of tiny home are seemingly endless. Because of all the variations and differences between them, it's hard to come up with a full troubleshooting checklist for every tiny home you may encounter. Two prefab houses or two THOWs may be so very different all while still having many of the options you've included in your list of wants and needs. This is why I highly recommend looking at as many as possible before you make your final purchase.

Above all, when it comes to choosing your very own tiny home, trust yourself. You know what you like. You know what you need. You will know if climbing up and down a ladder to go to the bathroom late at night is a good idea for you. There will be options that you look at and immediately say, "NOPE." If at all possible, take your time shopping around and drill down to get as much information as possible. If you don't have the option to visit the houses in person, look at as many pictures as you can, preferably those in which the home is staged to look like it's occupied. How many chairs fit in the seating area? How big is the refrigerator? Are there pictures of the bathrooms?

If you look at photos and cannot imagine yourself living in that space, then it is likely not the right space for you. Remember to include a link to photos in your notes and explain to yourself why you don't like it. This can make it so much easier to narrow down your choices in the long run, leading you to the ultimate logical decision.

In the next chapter, we'll look at considerations like land permits, mobility requirements, and details like insurance and utilities. These are all definitely parts of the tiny house experience that you'll need to consider before you make your final purchase.

There are so many moving parts and pieces to the tiny house equation that you may start feeling hopeless and defeated at times. This is absolutely normal. As noted at the beginning of this book, it's not a simple process, and you will have to do some legwork to make sure you're completely legal. However, every dream requires some dedication before it comes true. The information is out there, and there are plenty of individuals in the tiny home community who are more than happy to help you along the process. Resources are bountiful, and if you find yourself getting frustrated by dead ends, remember that there are so many different roads to try next. Let your notes and your dreams be your guide, and don't be afraid to reach out to others in the community to help you find your way.

CHAPTER 3: LAND, LOCATION, AND LEGAL CONSIDERATIONS OF TINY HOME DWELLING

Of course, having the ultimate tiny home of your dreams won't be entirely possible unless you have a place to put it. You'll also need to make sure you can pay for your house, that you can insure it as is required by your state or location, and that you can legally obtain the resources you need to make it run, like electricity, water, and heat.

This is also where most of the difficulties lie in the tiny house dilemma. You see, some areas have restrictions on how big or small a vehicle on wheels can be. Does it or can it come off of the trailer? Some locations consider them a mobile or trailer home, while others consider them RVs. In some places, it's not ok to park an RV at a trailer park and vice versa. Even if you own the land, there might be regulations about what's considered a permanent structure.

Then you get into the legal bits, like getting a mortgage or loan, and trying to insure the finished product. Is it a house or a temporary structure? Is it considered a recreational vehicle or a permanent dwelling? Do you insure the house and the trailer together or separately? Do you need a CDL (Commercial Driver's License) to tow it around? And, if so, does that mean you need to get commercial vehicle insurance? Is it even legal to haul on the freeways? Depending on your location and where you plan to go with your tiny house, the list can go on and on.

Therefore, it would be impossible to address every single if/then scenario when it comes to the legal implications of building, living in, moving, purchasing, and insuring a tiny house. Consider this a high-level overview of some of the things you might not have thought about when it comes to tiny house living. The ins and outs can be very complicated, and there may be overlapping and conflicting information, depending on your location.

While we can't give you all of the ins and outs for the exact tiny structure you want to live in, we can point you in the right direction for what to consider and where to go for more information. The links in the Resources section will guide you to great starting points, regardless of your location or destination. Additionally, the chapters in this section will help you learn how to ask the right questions in order to get all of the answers you need.

Section 1: Building on a permanent foundation

You might think, *well, if I own the land, then I can do whatever I want, right*? In some places that's true. Either the building codes and zoning laws for that area are very lenient, or the community has decided not to enforce them.

But if you've ever accidentally tangled with a Homeowner's Association (HOA) in the past, you'll know that some communities take these regulations very seriously, down to the tiniest pink flamingo.

Earlier, we discussed building codes. Generally speaking, most locations will want to know that any permanent structures being built meet the International Residential Code (IRC) and/or the International Building Code (IBC) requirements. The next thing you'll want to check are the Zoning Regulations. These can be mandated at the federal, state, and local level. You're likely familiar with some of the broader implications of zoning, which designates certain areas as residential, commercial, agricultural, and so on. But these guidelines can also require certain types and sizes of buildings on lots.

For example, some areas consider tiny houses to be an accessory dwelling unit (ADU). This might be the case if you're putting up a cottage or granny pod in addition to your current home but can prevent you from *exclusively* building a tiny house on your property. You may have to research ways to get around this, such as constructing a tiny house that meets the recommended square footage for a single-family detached dwelling in that county or township. Some folks have gotten around this requirement by constructing another structure, like a barn, workshop, or garage that meets the zoning laws. So while you may need to be creative, there are work-arounds. You just might need to be a little innovative. Again, this is why taking the time to do research is so very important.

Then there's the matter of utilities. Some localities require all single-family permanent structures to be attached to the municipal water sources and sewage system. Since part of the draw of having a tiny home is the ability to live off the grid, regulations such as these may cramp your style. On the other hand, that does mean you won't have to deal with the composting toilet, which might be a bonus, depending on the lists you made during the last chapter's soul-searching exercise. Of course, just because the connection exists doesn't mean you have to use it.

Remember the historic tiny homes we discussed in the previous chapter? Sometimes these get away with their existence due to homestead laws or historic building registries. Given the complications that would be involved in bringing these structures up to requirements that were established long after the dwelling was constructed, these homes tend to get a pass on zoning and code specifications. That's not a blanket statement, though, so always be sure to double-check, even if your prospective tiny home has actually been on its foundation since the beginning of time.

The following checklist should help you organize some of the requirements, restrictions, and legal nuances that you'll encounter when attempting to construct a tiny house on a foundation on your own land:

1. Locate the zoning requirements for your state, county, and township. You may need to consult with a building professional or do some digging on the local auditor's website. There are some leads to get you started in the Resources section of this book, but you're going to want to be very detailed here.
2. Double check the address of your land with the zoning map.
3. What are the local zoning requirements for a single-family detached home? Start at the state level, then the county level, then look at the requirements for the specific zoning code for your lot.
    a. What is the minimum permitted square footage?
    b. Can the home be constructed inside city limits?
    c. What building codes must be met for the structure?
    d. Is it considered the main building or an ADU?
    e. Will you need to hook up to utilities?
    f. What building codes are enforced in this area? (e.g., size of rooms, hallways, windows, ladders/stairs)
    g. How are these codes enforced?
4. Now, take a look at the tiny home prospects that meet your needs and wants. Which will work? Which will require modification? How difficult will these updates be?

This is another good time to pull out the notebook or journal to keep details organized. This checklist may look pretty straightforward, but there's a lot of fiddly details involved.

For example, in my home state of Ohio, tiny houses aren't specifically addressed on the state level, but at the local level, there are many variations on the requirements. In some areas, like metropolitan Cleveland, primary residences under 950 square feet are not permitted. You can have an ADU, but it can't be your permanent residence. In Oklahoma, however, tiny houses haven't even been addressed by zoning laws, so it's kind of a free-for-all. In some areas, including parts of Florida, entire tiny house communities have been established, where only tiny houses can be constructed, but then a few counties away from these tiny havens, you can't have a small detached residential structure at all.

This may seem like a lot of legwork, and to be honest, this is the most complicated part of transitioning to tiny home living. You may feel more comfortable consulting with a housing or building expert in your area to ensure you're looking at all of the right requirements correctly. The last thing you want is to have your dreams dashed because your loft ladder has the wrong tread width.

On the other hand, you might read this section and feel relieved that you're not interested in a permanent dwelling. Keep in mind, THOW regulations are just as complicated. Read on to find out how to keep your mobile tiny home legal.

Section 2: Considerations for a tiny house on wheels

In many places, a tiny house on wheels (THOW) is considered a recreational vehicle. However, this is not always true.

Therefore, if the THOW life is calling your name, the very first thing you should consider is the legality of the size and shape of the structure you are hoping to call home. In the previous chapter, we took a look at the idea of tiny house kits and professionally designed tiny houses. One of the major advantages we discussed is that these plans have already been vetted by professionals to be up to code.

When you have a THOW, you not only have to worry about where to park your recreational vehicle, but the matter of transportation becomes a concern. Typically, a tiny house that measures under 8 feet 6 inches wide, 13 feet 6 inches tall, and 40 feet long will meet the Department of Transportation trailer regulations without requiring a special permit. But that doesn't mean all of the roadways you wish to explore will be accommodating of those measurements. Low bridges, thick tree growth, and narrow back roads can make traveling with your tiny home extraordinarily treacherous.

Some THOWs are permanently constructed on a trailer base, such as the 84 Lumber kit mentioned in the previous chapter. Others are adapted to be moved with a trailer but can slide off and on the trailer rig, much like a traditional mobile home or a pop-up camper rig. Each version has its share of complications and benefits.

If it lives on a trailer full time, it's very likely your THOW will be considered an RV. That means you may encounter difficulties in parking it. The dimensions may not adhere to local RV park guidelines, especially if you have a loft or second level. At the same time, local ordinances may prevent owners from parking an RV on the plot of land you own for more than 30 days. There are designated RV parks around the country, many of which have space for permanent residents. However, these parks may have regulations surrounding tiny homes, despite the structure being legally defined as an RV in that area.

Mobile homes are typically defined as greater than 400 square feet in size and in most locations must have the wheels up, removed, or immobilized when parked. If your THOW is permanently attached to a trailer, this will be impossible. That may prevent you from being able to set up your new home in a mobile home park too.

Now, before you throw up your hands and give up, remember that you are not the only person who has ever encountered all of these seemingly endless, conflicting guidelines. There are plenty of places where tiny homes are welcomed or even ignored. Take a look at this chart with plenty of options to consider:

Option	Pros	Cons
RV Park/Tiny Home Community	• Will have the resources you need • Welcoming • Understands tiny house challenges • Sense of community	• May have parking limits • May be hard to locate • Not off the grid • Can be crowded • May have more rules and regulations to follow
Federal Land	• No one will disturb you • Completely off the grid • Fully legal • Can explore at will	• Can be hard to locate • May be impossible to get a THOW parked there • Still have regulations on length of stay
Rural Plot of Land	• You own the land • Off-grid in many aspects • Great way to be self-sustaining from a food aspect	• Still subject to property taxes • Zoning applies, but may be loosely enforced • Some utilities may be required • Limits ability to explore
Flying Under the Radar (aka: Doing What You Want)	• Park and travel however you want • Completely off-grid • Only have as much social immersion as you want • No land costs or parking fees	• Risky • Need to be aware of consequences • May require packing up and leaving immediately • May have legal/tax consequences

This list is not all-inclusive, of course, and depending on where you stay (or roam), the pros and cons may be more extensive. However, this should give you some perspective on the options that are available to you and some of the things to keep in mind when pursuing those options.

Another thing you'll need to keep in mind as a THOW-dweller is your tow vehicle. As someone who has done a lot of work for the automotive industry, I could go on all day about GVWR (Gross Vehicle Weight Rating - a detailed measure of the weight of a vehicle and everything in it) payload, towing capacity, horsepower and torque, and what to look for in a vehicle to tow your tiny home. At the end of the day, however, you're going to want to purchase a truck that you feel comfortable driving, that you can afford, and that makes sense for your lifestyle.

In fact, you may not want to buy a truck at all. When it comes time to move your THOW, you do have the option of renting a truck or contracting with a hauling company to move your home for you. These are going to be pretty pricey, of course, but if you have no reason to own a truck besides occasionally moving your tiny house, they would be far less expensive than letting a Heavy Duty truck sit around unused.

Depending on the size of your house, a half-ton truck may be sufficient. This includes models like the Ford F-150, the Silverado 1500, or the Toyota Tundra. However, if you are new to trucks, the number one thing you need to know is that not every model is going to have the same towing capacity. Oftentimes, the cab/bed configuration, axle ratios, and engine choices will impact the overall towing maximum. You'll also find different numbers for traditional hitches and gooseneck hitches. When searching for a truck, look specifically for the maximum towing figures and what configurations, options, or accessories are required to reach that number. Most full-sized trucks will offer a comprehensive towing package that will give you the best features and towing numbers possible.

If your tiny home size or weight requires a Heavy Duty truck, double check that you won't need a Commercial Driver's License (CDL) to operate it. In most cases, the truck itself can be operated with a regular driver's license but pulling an entire house behind it may change the game.

Always pay attention to the hitches. A traditional trailer isn't going to connect to a gooseneck and vice versa. There are also a wide variety of hitch classes and possibilities. You'll need to make sure the brake wiring and electric is properly connected too. Some trucks will be able to handle only a small portion of hitch classes, while others can take on a variety of loads. Ask questions about every truck on your list of options to ensure you've got the right equipment.

Cab size is another consideration if you have children or pets joining you. Many times, regular cab models will have the highest towing capacities, but these vehicles generally only seat two to three people. A larger cab with a backseat may make more sense for your lifestyle but can also compromise your towing capacity.

The good news is that this information is not difficult to find. A quick internet search of the year, make, and model will give you the towing specs. If you're buying a new or pre-owned truck from a dealership, you'll be able to discuss your towing requirements with the staff who will have all the figures you need to keep you and your tiny house safely on the road.

The last thing to briefly mention when it comes to hauling a THOW is the actual traveling itself. As mentioned earlier, narrow roads and low bridges may become problematic depending on the height of your THOW. But there are other practical implications of pulling a house—gas stations, for example.

A lot of fuel stops in the US have overhead roofs that may be an obstacle for a tiny house with a loft. Tight turns can also be cumbersome or even dangerous. Jackknifing is a real concern, and the aerodynamics of your tiny house may make driving in high winds or rain terrifying. Therefore, you may want to throw into your list of THOW considerations having to mpa out and preplan your routes to ensure safety along the way.

You'll definitely want to take the opportunity to learn how to drive with your trailer. Basically, this will require a lot of practice in a low-risk area. Additionally, you may look for trailer-friendly features in your tow rig. Modern trucks have all sorts of equipment on board to assist in trailering, from auxiliary switches that operate trailer lights and features, to cameras that help you see in and around the trailer as you drive. These features should not be considered cheating; instead, they are very important ways to keep you, your family, your home, and everyone on the road as safe as possible.

Section 3: The Legal Bits

I'm the type of person who really likes to take care of everything on my own. I love digging into the research and finding all the fussy details that make things work. That being said, there is absolutely nothing wrong with consulting with a professional when it comes to what I call "the legal bits" of tiny house ownership: the financing and the insurance.

Getting a loan in the United States isn't too terribly difficult. Even with bad credit or no credit, you can generally find a creditor to provide you with a sum of money, though the interest rate on said loan may take your breath away.

The good news is that tiny houses traditionally cost less than full-sized houses. In fact, you can build a tiny house for as little as $10,000 if you put your mind to it. However, that $10,000 space might not be perfect for you. Additionally, most of us don't have five to six digits worth of savings that we can wantonly spend, which means some type of lending or mortgage will be required to get fully invested in your tiny home.

Unfortunately, that drags us right back to the "is it a house or an RV?" question. RV loans exist but may not permit using the structure as a permanent dwelling until the loan is fully paid off.

You may be thinking, *well, they'll have to catch me and prove that I'm living there*. And that's true. That is a roll of the dice that some tiny home dwellers are willing to take, especially in the fly-under-the-radar style of living. It's risky, for sure, and the penalties differ depending on the lendor and the location.

You can also search for non-traditional lending. Besides crowdfunding opportunities, there are actually quite a few online investment methods that are based on non-traditional, private loans. Again, there are various levels of risk associated with these programs, and only you will be able to vet how comfortable you are with the risks and rewards.

Your best bet might be financing your tiny house as a primary or secondary residence. The requirements for these types of loans again vary between financial institutions, and you'll need to do some shopping around to find a loan that best fits your needs. Therefore, keep the following in mind when searching for the right loan for you:

- What is the interest rate?
- What does the monthly payment look like?
- What factors can impact the monthly payment?
- What is the loan period? (How long do you have to pay it off?)
- Does the lending party consider your tiny house an RV or a permanent structure?
- What's in the fine print?
- What are the stipulations of the loan and the consequences for disobeying these stipulations?

Remember, if you're buying a THOW, you might be looking at a loan for a truck to haul your prospective home in addition to purchasing the home itself. Is there a way to combine the financing through one institution? Frequently, auto dealerships provide their own financing for vehicles, but that doesn't mean you're required to use their resources. See what can be consolidated for the best rate and lowest monthly payment.

Frequently, the loan and the insurance go hand in hand. Naturally, if you're still making payments on the structure, your lender will want to know that they can recoup their money in the event of a disaster. The challenge comes in making sure your loan and your insurance match up.

You may need to explore a variety of options when it comes to insurance. Since your tiny house might be considered a recreational vehicle, you'll likely need to insure it as such. But RV insurance isn't intended to be insurance for a permanent dwelling either. The rates and coverage are based on infrequent use of a temporary residence. The greater the usage, the greater the risk. Therefore, you might need to look into a rider to provide additional coverage for the full extent of the structure and the contents.

If you're on a permanent foundation, it's more likely that you'll be able to finance and insure your tiny house as a primary residence, but the coverage still may not match the reality of the home. Property insurance is designed to cover liability and structural damage for a full-sized house and often is calculated based on square footage and construction materials. The goal is to be able to reproduce your house nail for nail and stud for stud, based on current market costs.

Property insurance also takes into mind the location of the house. Considerations such as weather risks (like tornados or hurricanes) and physical concerns (such as large trees that can blow over or uneven terrain) can impact your ability to get an insurance policy as well.

While all of this is pretty standard in the insurance industry, it can be a real pain if you're trying to fly under the radar with your tiny home. As a veteran of the insurance industry, I would recommend against trying to commit insurance fraud, however inadvertently, and be honest when you're working with the insurance company. You can actually save a lot of money, time, and frustration if you're up front with your agent or officer.

If you are going mobile, make sure you have coverage for the trailer and truck as well. Some states require trailer insurance in addition to RV insurance, but it's relatively inexpensive and provides more liability coverage during transit.

I also strongly recommend shopping around when it comes to insurance as well. Whether you're doing an online quote or sitting down in person with a representative, provide them with the structural details of your tiny house, including square footage and construction details. Be upfront about how you plan to use your tiny home, including how often you plan to travel, where you want to go, and whether you're going to be on or off-grid.

As I mentioned earlier, you might want to get a professional involved, especially if all of this is unfamiliar territory. There are tiny house experts who offer their services consulting on each and all of these topics. You'll want to make sure they're the real deal before you pay them for their services, and make sure you're comfortable with what they're doing. Additionally, there are plenty of guides and communities that can help you navigate the waters. Remember that every person is going to have a slightly different experience so take their advice with a grain of salt. Still, knowing you're not alone as you make these difficult decisions and conduct seemingly endless research can be immensely helpful throughout the process.

You may be feeling completely overwhelmed or frustrated at this point in the process and rightly so. But before you throw in the towel on your tiny house dreams, think about this objectively. Is it any more frustrating or strenuous than purchasing any other type of home? Are the complications in the process due to your unwillingness to compromise or from an external factor? If external, what type of accommodations can you make to work within the guidelines presented?

In the first chapter, we looked at all of the draws of tiny house living and your own hard and fast requirements for making it work. When you find yourself growing frustrated, consider visiting those lists or concepts again. Are your preferences evolving and changing as you go deeper and deeper down the rabbit hole? It very well might be that now is not the time for your tiny house adventure. You might need more time before you can make it happen the way you want, or more money, or a more accommodating location. Just like any other major transition in your life, a lot of things can change between the first inkling of an idea and the actual realization of your dream.

Therefore, I recommend you stay calm, stay organized, and when in doubt, research it out. Frustration comes from a place of emotional disruption, and while it's perfectly natural to have a lot of feelings about completely changing your living situation, the best way to combat these feelings is with facts and logic. You are absolutely allowed to cry and yell and fuss when things don't work out on the first try, just as you are encouraged to celebrate the victories along the way. However, when you feel you've hit a wall, take several deep breaths and head back to the drawing board with all of your facts in hand.

CHAPTER 4: SETTLING INTO A TINY HOUSE

Now, here's where we push the fast-forward button a bit. In the first chapter, we took a look at the pros and cons of tiny house living and completed a few exercises to help you determine if you're really ready to take the plunge into the tiny house lifestyle. Next, we looked at the different types of tiny houses and some of the advantages and challenges associated with each. Chapter 3 is intended to get your thoughts and questions sorted out when it comes to additional considerations about living in a tiny home and get you started down the relevant research path before you finalize your plans.

So then what happens? Slowly, but surely—or perhaps in a blazingly fast and furious sweep—you make all of your decisions. In my case, I had little input into our tiny house. It was there. We loved the set up. It was within our budget. Everything lined up much faster than I ever intended. But this is the exception, not the rule. In retrospect, I wish I had had enough time to prepare, because the next several months involved fiddling around a mostly unfurnished house with my husband, trying to figure out what we were doing, and where we were going with this endeavor. Time is a luxury, and if you can afford it, take as much as you can!

Once you have your plan settled, it's time to execute. That might mean printing out plans, buying supplies, and driving the first nail into your new home. It may mean driving your newly purchased truck out to hitch up your professionally constructed tiny home, ready to drag it to wherever you plan to spend your first night. It may even mean chasing out the bugs and rodents so you can move into your 1800s cabin. It all depends on how intrepid you are and what decisions make the most sense for you in the end.

Regardless of where your choices lead you, it is now time to pad your nest, so to speak, and establish the new patterns of your new lifestyle.

We've taken a look at how all of the space needs to be superfunctional, but what about the things you put in your home? The thing about the comforts of home is that they're supposed to be comfortable. But, in a tiny home, you don't have room for that overstuffed sectional or the king-sized therapeutic mattress. So how do you adapt?

Furthermore, you're going to have to do functional house stuff in order to sustain yourself—that means appliances and bath fixtures. Your tiny home may come with appliances, and if you've purchased a construction kit, you might have recommendations for what appliances you should put in there. But, as always, you do have a choice as to what to keep in your home. Plus, what do you do if you need to replace something?

Lastly, you've got to establish a flow in your home. This is going to take time and be largely experiential. You may find that the way you thought you would use your space is very much different from the way it actually works. However, the process can be a little more nerve-wracking than it typically is in larger houses.

You may be thinking, *I'm pretty sure I can figure out how to use my house without reading a book*, and I am completely confident that you can. However, making a transition from a larger house (where you can just close the bedroom door and stretch out on the bed for some private time) to a tiny house (where you have to climb up into the loft and do some light yoga to get into bed) can be a bit of a shock the first few times.

If you've grown accustomed to sacking out in front of the television after dinner every night, where are you going to do that now? Where are you going to put the television?

If you work from home, where are you putting your work area? What types of surfaces and seating do you need to get your job done, and how do you consolidate that with all of the other activities you do throughout the day?

I thought that living the van life would prepare me for tiny house dwelling. After all, I knew how to do a lot of stuff in a little space. However, it wasn't until we actually moved into our tiny house that Brad and I discovered that our van-life success had depended a great deal on having the outdoors to work with. Establishing outside areas can be helpful for your tiny house lifestyle as well.

The goal of this chapter is to help you consider all of your daily ins and outs so that you can adequately prepare your tiny home for your move-in day. There will always be a learning curve for figuring out how things work. No one can help you establish a flow; it just comes with time and experience. However, you can start thinking about some key elements of your lifestyle now and how to best reflect that lifestyle in the interior of your new tiny home.

Let's get started turning your new tiny house into your dream home!

Section 1: Furniture, Tiny-Style

We've already established that your full-sized eight-person dining table and sectional recliner sofa will most likely not fit in your tiny house, but the considerations for furnishing your new home don't stop there.

Take a look around at your current home. What kind of furniture do you have? You might have a dining table and chairs, a sofa, some side chairs, a coffee table, and perhaps some lamps. Try to adjust your gaze. Look at them from a perspective of not how useful or comfortable they are, but in regard to how much space they take up. Your everyday dining chairs may suddenly look enormous. Lampshades take up an incredible amount of space. Additionally, the square footage on your rugs may astound you.

Now, you can take measurements of all of your existing furniture to see how much square footage it actually takes up. For many people, that is an extremely helpful exercise. You can compare that to the actual measurements of your tiny house to figure out what will fit and what will not.

An option that's also effective but requires less math is to start with your floorplans and then consider your needs. Take a look at the actual space and then consider how furniture will actually fit. Or you can flip that and look at the space from the perspective of your needs, then determine what tools are needed to make that space do exactly what you need it to do.

Regardless of how you approach your furnishings, you're going to need to consider size, shape, and function, not just of the furniture, but of your overall space. There's a bit of a jigsaw-puzzle feeling when attempting to make the whole equation work. This is why furnishing a tiny house is much more challenging to many people, compared to a regular-sized dwelling.

Start with the part of the house that's most important to you. If having a cozy area where you can rest and relax is most important to you, start in the bedroom. If creating and enjoying home cooked meals is a priority, start with the kitchen and dining area. If you know that you're going to lose productivity unless you've strategically created the perfect workspace, then start there.

I truly do recommend approaching this like a jigsaw puzzle, trying out different pieces in different areas to see if they have that *just right* fit. Let's say you know you want a flat surface for your laptop, and you need a chair that's going to provide back support while you work. So you start with the workstation. Consider that the flat surface you use for work can also be used as your dining space. What area has the best lighting so you don't have to squint at your computer screen? Is there room for the chair you need there? Can that chair also function as a lounge chair in the evenings? Or is there another area more suitable for lounging?

As you can see in this example, the puzzle pieces flow from one area to another. Everything is connected in a tiny house, because you can't just tuck your office chair in a corner when you're not using it.

For another example, let's look at the 84 Lumber "Countryside" model, which was House #4 in Chapter 2, Section 3. Please note that I'm not specifically endorsing this model. I've never seen it in person, and I have no ties with 84 Lumber or any of its affiliates. This particular tiny house has won several accolades for its design, so I've done a lot of analysis regarding what works in this particular plan.

One thing that stands out in the living space of this model is that it's equal parts living space and kitchen. The kitchen may be in small, RV-like proportions, but all of the traditional components are there, from appliances, to sink, to countertops.

Take a look at the living space. There's a high countertop along the windows that can be used as a desk or eating space. Directly across from that is a bench-style daybed with under-seat storage. This could serve as a lounging/sofa-type area, or you could pull up a TV tray and eat there or work there; this is truly a flexible living space that can serve multiple purposes.

In this type of floor plan, the only furnishings you would really need are chairs for the dining and work-surface space as well as a bed for upstairs. The design of the floor space in this particular model really limits your ability to add things like chairs and coffee tables, though, on the plus side, the built-ins cover many needs.

Compare this, then, with some of the other plans you can find online. Some might have fewer built-ins in the living area, which means you have greater flexibility for creating your own dining/working/lounging space. Some tiny houses may have one large room, while others have a separate flex room/area where you can set up an office, second bedroom, movie room, or whatever your lifestyle requires.

Does tiny house living mean you'll have to throw out all of your furniture and start over? Well, yes and no. There are some things that will clearly not fit. There are some things that you can reasonably make work. Moreover, there are other furnishings and fixtures that will make the transition with you perfectly.

In the next chapter, we'll look at the process of minimizing and keeping your lifestyle minimized. But, for now, prepare to part ways with some of your larger furnishings, either through donation or yard sale. While this can be bittersweet, it's an important step in writing the next chapter of your life.

Section 2: Appliances and Fixtures

If you are purchasing a prefabricated tiny home of any sort, or you've purchased a kit that includes appliance recommendations, this part will already be decided for you. Your kitchen and bathroom will already come equipped with plumbing, electricity, and the fixtures necessary to cook and keep yourself clean.

That being said, you may need to replace those at some point in the future. Whether you change your mind regarding the types of appliances and fixtures that came with the tiny house, or something breaks, or you end up wanting to make your free-wheeling lifestyle more permanent, there may come a time that you need to look for new appliances and fixtures.

It's also worth noting that if you're building your own tiny house, you'll be looking for these items for the first time.

It can be kind of intimidating, shopping for tiny appliances. This is one instance in life where size really matters. Not only do you have to make sure that the appliance or fixture fits in the spot where you want to put it, but you need to make sure that it has the ability to function properly with your electric and plumbing set up.

In our tiny house, we have a regular-sized microwave, a small refrigerator that fits perfectly under the kitchen counter, and a one-cup coffee machine. We have three overhead lights downstairs and one lamp upstairs. We also have two outlets for charging laptops, phones, and devices, and a furnace that provides intermittent heat when the temperature drops below a certain level. We specifically chose these items conscientiously with the capacity of our roof-mounted ceiling panels in mind.

When it comes to electricity and plumbing, your tiny house may be very similar to a camper, motorhome, or other RV. Unless you're built on a permanent foundation, or the zoning requirements indicate you must be hooked up to the local sewer and power grid, you have a lot of freedom in this regard.

Living off-grid is a very large part of the tiny house draw, especially for those who elect to put their house on wheels. Since utilities are often a huge part of our monthly expenses, whether we rent or own our homes, transitioning into a tiny house is going to create a fantastic opportunity for savings. The limited opportunities for using power and water are going to drastically reduce your need for these commodities.

Even if you do end up staying at least partially on the grid, you're going to notice a big difference in your utility expenses. After all, you can now theoretically light your entire home with a single light bulb.

So now it's time to continue making decisions to fill your house with the necessities. Are you going to have electricity in your tiny house, and if so, where is it going to come from?

Most THOW setups have either a generator system or solar panels. There are pros and cons for each power source. Generators can be loud and require fuel, which can disrupt the whole green living concept you might be going for. They also require maintenance and attention to ensure they're running safely and correctly over time. Still, they can be very helpful for providing long-term reliable power, especially if you're going to keep a variety of devices charged.

Solar panels require no fuel, are generally pretty silent, and aside from checking on them from time to time to ensure they're still properly fastened to your roof or walls, require no maintenance. On the other hand, they are pretty expensive to install, and when they stop working, the panels have to be completely replaced rather than repaired. You may not have power on demand, either, if you choose to park your THOW in an area that's shady, rainy, or if you need to work during the dark hours.

There is, of course, the little-bit-of-both option, in which you install solar panels, but bring along a generator for those just-in-case times. This can be a little easier in a tiny house setup than in other forms of RVs, depending on how frequently you plan to move your THOW.

Ultimately, the type of appliances you choose will need to be suitable for your power source. It may be difficult to run a full-sized refrigerator on the number of solar panels you can fit on a tiny house. Take stock of your actual electrical needs. Are there places where you can choose a non-electric power source?

Your phone and laptop will likely require a power source to keep them charged. How about your refrigerator? Cook top? Water heater? Electric kettle? Will you need or use fans or heaters to keep your tiny house cool or warm, depending on the weather outside? Are you going to have a television, radio, or projection screen? What about an alarm clock? There are so many ways that we use electricity without thinking about it, which makes it very important to have these appliances considered before you move into your house and need to re-think some crucial requirements.

If you can live without electronic devices, then consider yourself quite lucky, and move on to your lighting. Tiny houses can be designed to have plenty of windows for natural light, but there are a few tricky spots. First, if you are in an area that is cold or windy, your windows may impact how warm you can keep the inside of your dwelling. Then you'll have to think about a heating source, which might also require electricity. And, of course, natural light is not always available. Though there are some areas that experience 24 hours of sunlight from time to time, there will be darkness and dimness nearly everywhere you roam.

Battery-operated lights, such as flashlights and tap lights, can be very helpful, especially in small areas that don't need a lot of light, such as the bathroom or sleeping loft. Battery-operated appliances and tools are becoming increasingly prevalent, so it's very likely that many of the resources you need are available without a plug. You'll need to stock up on batteries, of course, but if your usage is minimal, this is a pretty cost-effective off-the-grid solution to creating light in the dark.

Lanterns, wood burning stoves, and propane camp stoves are excellent non-electric solutions for your household, as well, but remember that open flames and small spaces aren't always the best mix. Make sure you have plenty of ventilation, as well as the appropriate fire extinguishing equipment when using these types of tools. An external cooking area, such as a grill or a firepit, can be another solution to cooking without electricity.

If you do choose to set up your kitchen with appliances that require electricity, be conscientious about how much power you can use at once and how much each appliance requires. Some tiny houses have real-and-true kitchens with gas stoves and ovens, while others have electric burners built into the counters. Always check your load capacity and make sure that it's alright to run the electric kettle, the burners, and charge your phone at the same time. Otherwise, you'll plunge into darkness with cold water, cold dinner, and limited phone capability.

Refrigeration without electricity is possible though somewhat tricky. Brad and I used an old-fashioned ice chest in the van, which did the trick and kept things cool. On the downside, we've melted a lot of ice, and we've definitely lost a lot of delicious food due to water leaking into containers or ice melting faster than we could replace it. Unless you'll be moving around a lot, and thus have constant access to ice, I wouldn't necessarily recommend the ice chest method. Thankfully, you can find refrigerators in nearly every size and power supply, from those that can stay cool with a charge from the car battery to under-counter RV and dorm-sized units that can pack a surprising quantity of supplies for the size.

Then there are the fixtures that require water, such as sinks, showers, and toilets. Another thing to consider is laundry. Some tiny houses have room for a miniature washer and dryer, but those will require both electricity and a water source. You may prefer using laundromats or washing your clothes by hand and air drying them whenever possible. One quick note about that: there are some areas where using an outdoor clothesline is prohibited. While you're looking at zoning details, double check to see if there are any requirements for clotheslines before you accidentally put your unmentionables out for all to see!

Unless you are connected to a foundation and public water/sewer system, you will be using water tanks. Much like in any other type of RV, you'll have your dirty water, your greywater, and your freshwater tanks. That means you'll need a source for your fresh water, whether that's through rain collection sources or from the public spout in your tiny house community.

The good news is that these types of water systems have very few costs associated with them. Once you've purchased the tanks and have a reliable source of fresh water, you're pretty much good to go. You'll need regular maintenance to ensure all of the pipes and pumps are functioning properly, and you definitely need to stay on top of managing your black water and greywater tanks, but this type of system is definitely an "it is what it is" type of scenario.

Speaking of "it is what it is," there are some sacrifices that must be made when it comes to water usage. Using a composting toilet may take some getting used to. Putting a time limit on your showers may require some adjustment as well.

For me, washing dishes by hand has never become easier, though I may be perpetually in mourning for my full-sized dishwasher. Still, you will very quickly become more aware of how many dishes you are using and ensuring they're washed as soon as you're done using them. Between the clutter, the smell, and the bugs and rodents that appreciate a good crusty plate, the consequences of not cleaning up as soon as you're done with a meal will become immediately obvious.

The final thing you'll need to consider is how you're going to pack all of these utilities away. In a standard-sized house, you generally have a basement or designated utility room where your hot water tanks, fuses/breakers, and furnace are stored. Depending on what options you choose for your power and water sources, you'll need a place to store your generator, water tanks, and more.

In our home, that's all stashed under the stairs with the composting toilet. It is a very tight squeeze. We have debated moving the toilet into the shower shed, but the idea of dashing out of the house and across the lawn in the middle of the night is equally unappealing. You would think that living in a van for as long as we did would have hardened us, but there are some aspects of our suburban upbringing that we haven't quite reconciled with our lifestyle and passions yet.

Once you have the furnishings and fixtures determined, it's time to make it all functional. That means taking a look at your space and figuring out how it will work for you. That also means creating an aesthetic that makes you feel like you're at home without cluttering up the place.

Section 3: Balancing Function and Finishes

I am a firm believer that your home should reflect what you need and want it to be. As a writer, I need my space to be quiet yet inspirational. I need separate areas for focusing on my work as well as for relaxing. I see a blank wall as a threat, not a peaceful, meditative area. I like unique, colorful artwork that takes my mind and my imagination on wild journeys, but I also appreciate endless views into nature.

In a tiny house, there's not a lot of extra space for knickknacks, artwork, or colorful expressions of personality, but it's not impossible. There are plenty of ways to incorporate your personality and self-expression with regular functionality.

In our home, for instance, the internal bracing of the slatted cabin walls creates natural shelving areas where we can stash our collection of books.

All of our furniture has built-in storage as well. Our tables are made from old wooden shipping crates, so the plates and cutlery live inside the dining table. The crate we use as a coffee table holds toilet paper and cleaning supplies.

As a creative type, I think art belongs everywhere. From the throw pillows to the furniture, I love incorporating bright, bold colors. While bold colors might not be your thing, I do encourage you to use every possible outlet for self-expression: your countertops, your rugs, your pillows and bed sheets, your towels, and even the stain or paint you use on your wood surfaces. All of these are opportunities for a little personalization.

Some people feel that hanging artwork in a tiny house is competing with nature, but I find this to be a matter of personal taste. I love nature, and I very much cherish having the ability to take in some breathtaking views. But, at the same time, I have a lot of handmade art that is very meaningful to me. My plants are in pots made by my friend Eve, and some of them hang from macrame gifted to me by my friend Jess. These plants not only provide inspiration and create bright, cheerful spots in my home, but they hold the memories I've created with my loved ones. Plus, they do their part to keep the air fresh and clean in our tiny space.

Yes, it is easy to quickly overwhelm your tiny living area with too much art, but I think that it's very possible to demonstrate your aesthetic in functional pieces.

Another concept that you may wish to embrace is relocating the furniture between day and night. If you've ever been in a large RV, you'll know that many are equipped with seating areas that fold out into beds or benches that push out mechanically to become sleeping areas. You can apply that same convertible vibe to your tiny house with the right furnishings.

In our home, the tiny loveseat is actually a twin-sized foldout bed. We have two easy chairs upstairs that have tiny little nesting ottomans that tuck under the seat, which can be stacked on top of each other and stashed in the corner before we pull out the Murphy bed. We have a large old steamer trunk that is a closet for hanging clothes when placed on the short end but can also hold sheets and blankets when in a regular, flat position.

You can even create a balance between storage and display. Think about things that you use regularly, like dish towels or coffee cups. If you have a fun collection, you may wish to keep these items out in the open and incorporate them into your decor, rather than trying to find a suitable place to stash them when they aren't in use. You've likely seen the open-cabinet design in magazines or on home and decorating television shows. That's another type of storage that also works as a display.

As you examine the potential furnishings for your tiny home, look not only at the fit but the function. The tiny house lifestyle is all about possibilities and potential and finding opportunities to make things work without taking up a lot of space or resources. Innovation is key, and it can actually be fun to discover new ways to pad your nest without taking up space.

I don't want to overstep my boundaries and tell you how to decorate your home, but I will encourage you to personalize your space so that it feels very comfortable and conducive to what you need in a home. Therefore, my "Rules of Decor" are quite simple:

1. Don't be afraid to express yourself.
2. Consider your natural views and lighting.
3. Put the "fun" into "function" with multi-purpose furniture.
4. Examine every angle and how space and stuff can fit multiple scenarios (such as daytime/nighttime furniture arrangement).
5. Strike a balance between storage and display.

As mentioned throughout this book, this is your dream home. While compromise will be required to some extent, don't let yourself get swept into feelings of **well, this is how it has to be**. You do have a choice in this process, in fact, as we've discovered throughout the chapters, you have many choices.

It can be overwhelming. You may come to a point of saying "whatever" and just going with it. I speak from experience here, since Brad and I were very limited in our choices prior to moving into this particular tiny home. There are many, many things I would do differently if I were purposefully building my own dream tiny home. Not only is hand-washing dishes a point of contention for me, but I also wish the porch was on the back of the house, instead of the front, so I could watch sunsets. It's the little things that mean something in the long run.

But there are equally plenty of things that I have learned from living in this home. There are features that I never thought I could deal with that I actually love, such as having a tiny refrigerator that I have to sit on the floor to pack and unpack. I'm very limited in what I can put in there, and so we've been resisting the temptation to buy food we don't need. Our grocery bill has never been smaller. Thanks to the amazing windows in this house, I have gone days without switching on a lightbulb. Even if we didn't have solar panels, our electricity bill would be next to nil.

It's been a process of discovery, which is why I encourage everyone to keep their minds and their thoughts open. Discovering little ways to make a tiny space feel big is part of the fun. Try not to rush through the process, and let yourself uncover new magic in your new home every day.

CHAPTER 5: *MINI-MIZING YOUR LIFESTYLE*

The next part of the tiny house lifestyle I'd like to address is the day-to-day stuff you might not have thought of yet. From figuring out how to fit your life into a tiny house, to keeping it clean and organized, feeding yourself, and even making room and time for your pets or children, there are a lot of things that took me by surprise when I moved into a tiny house.

You would think that I'd be super-prepared, given that I had been living in a van, but honestly, it was a little confusing. Some parts, like walking to another building to shower, were very familiar. Other parts were deceptively convenient, like having a furnace in cooler weather and having an actual bedroom with a full-sized bed instead of a futon mattress in the back of a van. I say "deceptively," because it's all well and good until you run out of solar power, or you need to change the bedsheets and bang your head multiple times on the steeply angled ceiling beams.

In a regular-sized house, apartment, or condominium, you generally have closets or shelves of some sort to help you stash your stuff. Before I married Brad, I actually lived in an apartment that had a closet door that opened to reveal two additional closets. We learn to take abundant storage space for granted. If it's not built in, we simply run to IKEA or The Container Store and casually set up the freestanding storage unit that fits the space and the needs.

In van life, storage is at a premium, but it's very possible to create space for various-sized bins, containers, and in fancier rigs, drawers and cupboards. We managed to make it across the country several times with six drawers, three large flat bins, two bathroom buckets, and a cooler, which served as our clean clothes, dirty clothes, kitchen, pantry, cleaning-supply storage, medicine cabinet, and refrigerator.

But when we moved into the tiny house, the paradigm shifted entirely. We had kitchen drawers and cabinets built in under the sink as well as a small antique sideboard. As mentioned earlier, the kitchen table, coffee table, and other pieces of furniture were designed for storage. A small antique chifforobe was placed upstairs on the tall side of the room, and various shelves and cubbies were available throughout, thanks to the network of exposed studs and supports.

To fast forward to the good part, we're still using the van as a storage vessel. The bins, which fit neatly under our bed in the van, are too big for the tiny house. The bed isn't elevated in the house, due to the low ceiling, so we can't tuck them there. Instead, we've been putting our seasonal clothing in the chifforobe, and the off-season clothing is stored in the van.

Our cleaning products and bathroom essentials can live in the shower house. There are a few shelves in there, but they do get wet when the shower is on, so we needed to find a way to store our linens and towels in the house itself. Brad had the brilliant idea of putting them all in spare pillowcases and stacking them neatly in the corner. I must admit that I've used a pillowcase full of clean towels as a lounging floor pillow from time to time. In a tiny house, nearly everything has multiple purposes!

As you make the transition, you'll probably have several moments where you're absolutely overwhelmed by how little fits in your new space. Before you throw everything out except a single spoon (a threat I've made many times), I'd like to give you some pointers and advice. I know that these tips won't work for everyone, but I hope I can take just an ounce of anxiety or stress out of your tiny home transition.

Section 1: Reducing possessions and clutter

Let's start with *the stuff*. Your plan of action at this point might be, "Chuck it all. Start over." You are certainly empowered to do that, since it's your stuff, your life, and your money, but what if we dialed it back a few notches and made some smart decisions about your belongings?

Earlier, I recommended noting what furniture absolutely won't work, what might be able to work, and what is very much essential to your lifestyle and well-being. You're going to need to do this with your personal stuff too.

By "stuff," I honestly mean everything—from your books to your lamps and your cooking utensils to your computer monitor and towels. You've already accepted that the knickknacks, geegaws, thingamajigs, and thingamabobs alike will need to hit the road, but you probably didn't think about your wardrobe, the contents of your medicine cabinet, and your carefully cultivated collection of board games.

Again, do not panic. If you're like me, perhaps your heart just skipped a beat when you considered how huge this move is really going to be. But take this opportunity to look around at all of the people who have made the same exact transition that you're about to make. It can be done. It will be done, and you're going to be fine.

Also, before I inspire any more stress or panic, I'd like to take the opportunity to share with you that many people who live in tiny houses have a storage unit stashed somewhere. Even those who are constantly on the move in their THOWs will likely have their Great-Aunt Linda's bedroom set, or their far-too-meaningful-to-part-with collection of primitive cat art tucked away somewhere. I actually have an indoor storage locker in Ohio crammed full of original art created by my friends and family (and me, if I'm being honest!). I have absolutely no room for it, but I will not part with it until I shuffle off of this mortal coil. Therefore, I spent $15 a month for a temperature-controlled locker. If you have the budget and the desire, you are very much allowed to keep the larger things that are very meaningful to you, so don't despair that you'll never see your family heirlooms again.

With that in mind, let's take a look at your stuff. I've created this handy room-by-room chart to give you an idea of some of the things I'm talking about when it comes to "stuff." Please note, this chart is not to be considered all inclusive, by any means, and is merely provided to get your mind organized regarding your stuff. Objects are presented in no particular order.

Location	"Stuff"
Bathroom	Towels, linens, dental-care products, skin-care products, nail-care equipment, razors/personal grooming equipment, hair-care products (including appliances like curling irons, blow dryers, etc.), first-aid kit, toilet paper, menstrual products, trash bin, air freshener, cleaning supplies, rags, paper towels, sponges, bathmat, make up, mirrors
Bedroom	Linens, pillows, blankets of various sizes/thickness, bedside stand, reading lights, television, books, laundry bins, rugs, books, magazines, more skin-care products, nighttime pain relievers, nighttime indigestion assistance, heating pad
Kitchen	Bowls, plates, pots, pans, skillets, griddles, baking sheets and tins, casserole dishes, mugs, glasses, plastic cups, measuring cups, measuring spoons, stirring spoons, serving spoons/ladles/tongs, coffee maker, teapot, filters, reusable container collection, strainer, spatula, trays, napkins, clean-up liquid, sponges, rags, drying rack, toaster, toaster oven, waffle maker, popcorn maker, can openers, bottle openers Also, the food itself: cans, boxes, bags, refrigerated items, dry goods, snack foods, produce, frozen foods
Living Areas	Pillows, blankets, television, books, DVD player, DVD collection, games, puzzles, stereo equipment, CD/record collection, photo albums, framed pictures, souvenirs, candles, coasters, floral arrangements

Office	Desk, computer, mouse, keyboard, monitor, filing system, day planner, pens/pencils, art supplies, printer, printer paper, project/crafting table, craft supplies, chair, exercise equipment, video-game consoles, video games and equipment
Wardrobe/Clothes/Closets	Coats, jackets, pants, shirts, dresses, sweaters, ties, casual wear, pajamas, footwear, sweeper, mop, broom, buckets

It is clear from this chart that some simplification is in order for most of us, especially when heading into a tiny house.

Types of Organization Perspectives

I recommend approaching the minimization process with a purpose-driven perspective. That is, think of what purpose each item serves in your life. If it's something you reach for often, then by all means, make sure it's always within your reach. If it's something that means a lot to you, but you rarely touch it or interact with it, maybe it can head to storage. If you genuinely forgot you had it, feel free to give it a new lease on life through donation or a yard sale.

Of course, most people require a more thoughtful and disciplined approach than I typically take to organization. Therefore, I have a few methods you might appreciate as you attempt to de-clutter your lifestyle and rank your belongings by necessity and want. I have included links in the Resources section to help you learn more about organization as well.

1. **The Capsule Format** - You may have heard of "Capsule Wardrobes." I'm a huge fan of the concept because I'm not very good at coming

up with exciting outfits, and van living has taught me to exist with the absolute bare minimum.

The Capsule concept means stripping down your closet to your bare minimums. You'll keep only the things you wear most often and that can be worn in a variety of situations. This can also be applied to your belongings. Do you have a throw blanket that you love to snuggle with absolutely anywhere? Bring it. Can your throw pillows be used as floor seating? Excellent. Can your dining table also be your desk? Can your desk chair also function as a dining chair or a lounge chair? See how many purposes you can create for as many items as possible.

2. **Traditional Minimalism** - There are actually a lot of interpretations of minimalism, but in its purest form, it means getting rid of anything that isn't 100 percent necessary for daily survival: One spoon. One fork. One knife. One plate. It's a very spartan lifestyle that leaves no room for excess or expression.

Many people find this type of lifestyle freeing, for the same reason they find tiny house dwelling relieving. Tiny living means less stuff. Less stuff means less burden. Less burden means less worry, less responsibility, less aptitude for unnecessary curation of collections, and so on.

You actually don't appreciate how much of your brain is wrapped around your stuff until it's not there anymore. Even if you don't think about the fourteen folding chairs in your hallway closet, you know about them. And once they're gone? You'll feel free from those fourteen folding chairs. You'll never have to move them again. You'll never have to set them up and take them down again. You won't have to worry about one of them breaking right before a big family dinner. You don't have to learn how to repair them or figure out how to replace them. They are gone.

However, there are various degrees of minimalism. Some people choose an area of their life to simplify, such as their wardrobe, their bookcases, their kitchen accessories, etc. Many people are currently hooked on Marie Kondo's concept of "sparking joy." If you don't love it, it's time to part ways with it.

3. **Systematic Reduction** - This type of organization is a process rather than a one-and-done method. If you have a lot of time before you need to worry about packing to move into your tiny house, this is a great way to be sure that you've chosen wisely.

In this process, you set up boxes or bins in each room of the house you're planning to reduce (in this case, all of them). Each time you find something that you've completely forgotten about, put it in the box or bin. Continue this process every day over a span of time—you can start now, if you feel like you've got a lot of stuff to spare—and watch what happens. Notice how often you have to dig through your boxes to find something you need.

Systematic reduction uses the "out of sight, out of mind" principle, which is generally how we end up with a lot of stuff in the first place. I will confess that I did this before our van trip, and I discovered that we had nine bottle openers. They just kept accumulating, because we couldn't find the previously purchased opener. It was truly absurd, but this is the type of thing we, as humans, tend to do when we have a lot of space.

4. **"If it fits" Organization** - This is a really specific type of organization that some of my fellow van friends taught me, but it very much makes sense in the tiny house lifestyle. In this concept, you measure all available space, and you only bring what will fit.

   This is a very orderly method and requires a lot of analytical thought and logic to really pull it off, but it makes a lot of sense for those building their own tiny home. If you absolutely know that your largest storage space is eleven inches tall, then that cuts back on a lot of the possibilities. You can spend some time trying to figure out how to make it work or move on to finding a smaller option that will work immediately and without much creativity.

5. **The List** - This sounds like something from a sitcom, but it's very effective, especially if you feel you're not making any progress in your minimization efforts.

   The premise is very simple. Grab a box. Open a drawer, open a cupboard, closet, etc. Pull out the notebook or journal that you started. Write down every single thing you see in that spot. Now, at this step, you can either walk away and consider the list, or just go for it and pull the things you don't want or need out of the drawer, cupboard, or closet, and throw it in the box. Give the box a number and jot down that same number on the list.

If you end up needing that item, you'll know exactly where it is. In some cases, just knowing that you didn't want it originally will be enough to allow you the peace to give it up. In other cases, you'll realize you were being overzealous, and you really did need that thing. Either way, you can keep track of your process and progress with a list such as this.

Honestly, there's no bad way to get the ball rolling in organizing your home to prepare for the move to tiny. These are just five methods that have gained popularity among those transitioning to living tiny.

Another thing to keep in mind is that you don't have to live in a tiny house to practice any of these organization concepts. If you're reading this chapter, and you're feeling very anxious, you might not be quite ready to go tiny. Sure, tiny house living will force you to live a much more simplistic lifestyle, but if the actual process of reducing your collection is causing you physical or emotional pain, it may not be the right time. As I've said before, it's best to not do this in a rush, because it is a huge change in lifestyle.

You're not going to be able to fill a closet with toilet paper rolls and have room for your favorite floor steamer. And, if you do, you'll have to sacrifice something else. I've said that tiny house living is about imagining possibilities and being creative, but there truly is a lot of sacrifice involved.

On the other hand, this may be exactly the sign you needed to move forward with your plans. If you're the type who can pack for a weekend trip in a single reusable grocery bag, then you're set. For many people, the lessened financial burden and smaller carbon footprint draw them into the tiny house, but the simplicity of the lifestyle keeps them there.

As you work on organizing and minimizing, be honest with yourself. How do you feel? Energized? Excited? Eager? Restless? Regretful? Confused? All of these are valid emotional responses to any big transition in life, but overall, you should feel more positive emotions than negative. Pay attention to any red flags your mind tries to give you at this time.

Additionally, as you're getting rid of things, remember that there are a lot of options and opportunities for your old stuff. Check around your town for charities that accept lightly used items. Are there any book banks or libraries that might take the books you no longer need? Are there any local schools or after-school programs that can use discarded games, art and craft supplies, or DVDs? Sometimes, thinking about the next life that your old stuff will have takes the pain away from seeing it leave.

Local online sales walls are also a good option for getting rid of your possessions. Porch pickups can be a fast way to move your belongings. Always exercise caution when meeting people in person or conducting cash transactions via the internet, but if you're just looking for a good home for your stuff, this can be a great way to liquidate.

Oftentimes, preparing for a tiny house transition has a lot more steps than we imagine. Getting rid of your stuff and preparing for the simple lifestyle that comes with having less room can be emotional and difficult on many levels. Still, many people feel a great mental release once they unburden themselves from their unnecessary stuff. Take some time here to make sure you follow an organization process that makes sense for you in order to free yourself from the added stress of "breaking up" with your belongings.

Section 2: Keeping your tiny house clean

When you live in a tiny space, any size mess can be a big problem. From odors to insects, it's important to take care of your tiny home.

One of my tiny house tutors told me to think of my new home like a car. Say you're running some errands, and you have a drink in the cup holder. You stopped by the mailbox, and your mail is on your front seat. As you run errands, you put some stuff in the trunk. It's safely stashed back there, not rolling around as you drive. You run some more errands, and now you have some packages in your backseat. Then you pick up your spouse from work. You have to move the mail to the backseat, too, where it gets shuffled under the packages. Also, your spouse was awesome enough to get you a coffee when they bought their own, so now you have three drinks for two cup holders. It becomes a juggling act.

But the second act is what's really important. Let's say your spouse is chomping on some popcorn, too, as an after-work snack. You hit a pothole, and popcorn festively flies everywhere.

When you get home, you can either prioritize unloading the car by what you need most urgently, or you can take the time to empty the trunk, get the packages out of the backseat, fish the mail out from under the front seats, clean up the popcorn, remove all of the beverages, and check for any additional spills.

A lot of us do the bare minimum, thinking we'll take care of the rest later. That's generally because we don't immediately have to deal with the consequences of a car full of clutter and mess. But the next morning, that coffee is going to smell mighty funky. You may have a new family of mice feasting on the popcorn. Months go by, and you start to get late payment notices on the mail that snuck under the seats. Various cataclysmic events occur because you didn't take the time to tidy your car.

The metaphor is spot on. The smells, the clutter, the lost items that were hiding in a stack—it can all happen very quickly in a tiny house.

Now, this doesn't mean you can't take a day off from cleaning here and there. It just means if you are not a naturally tidy person, you will need to work on that in order to successfully pull off the tiny house lifestyle.

Whether you live on a fixed foundation or in a THOW, the bug struggle is real. Any morsel on the counter or sticky spot on the floor is a beacon for critters. Ants and mosquitos are particularly cunning and will use any excuse to come live with you for as long as possible.

How do you plan to clean your tiny house? There are a few concepts that you probably haven't considered if you're used to living in a regular-sized house.

First, ventilation. I'm not saying you can't use ammonia or bleach in a tiny house, but I am saying that you will want all of the windows open for several days after, if you do. "Green" cleaners, or those without harsh odors and chemicals are a great option for tiny spaces for this reason.

Next, your power supply. A lot of us rely on electricity and running water to clean our homes. If you do not plan to have utilities in your tiny home, realize that you are going to need to clean everything by hand. In many cases, that's no big deal—a quick push with the broom out the front door, a hand-scrubbing of all surfaces, and done. However, this can be a big deal if you have any mobility issues, awkward spaces where you can't fully stand up or squat down on your knees, or if you have pets (more on that in a moment).

Then there's the storage of your cleaning products. You definitely don't want to put the detergent in with the meat, so to speak. You'll want to make sure you have an area, preferably something with a door or lid to keep it closed off from air, moisture, and insects, where you can stash your cleaning products. That includes everything from your surface cleaner and disinfectant to your broom or electric sweeper.

The good news is that you'll have less space, which means you'll spend less time each day cleaning and use fewer cleaning products. You'll be able to save plenty of money on cleaning supplies. You may find that your time spent cleaning increases, though, with necessity driving a higher frequency.

What about garbage? Sure, lots of things can be composted or gathered and taken to public recycling. And, if you don't have a lot of stuff, then you likely won't have much to throw away. Waste not, want not, right? Still, many of us manage to accumulate at least a little bit of waste that cannot be composted or recycled.

If you have a THOW, or you're trying to live under the radar, curbside trash service isn't going to be a possibility. Some towns and villages have public dump sites, where you can easily toss a bag or two of your waste into a large dumpster or container. If flying under the radar really is your thing, then you might be pretty good at dropping things off at a gas station or fast-food restaurant as you cruise by. On the other hand, if you're living on a fixed foundation, you might be able to sweet talk your neighbors into letting you borrow a little trash bin space here and there.

But expand the concern a bit: How are you going to gather trash within the tiny house—all of your used tissues, empty soup cans, shredded junk mail, sanitary products, etc. Where are you going to put them until you can properly dispose of them outside of your house? Again, there are odors to deal with and the possibility of attracting bugs and animals. Mice absolutely love it when we humans make donations of easily accessible, shreddable paper.

A small trash can with a lid is a great idea, especially if you can station it easily by the door for immediate removal. Remember, if you put anything outside, it will be summarily inspected in detail by any critter that wanders by, from the neighbor's dog to the local group of raccoons. You likely do not want trash strewn across your lawn, especially if you're trying to be discreet or have found a tiny house community that you really enjoy.

Disposing of everything immediately isn't merely a good idea in a tiny home—it's an absolute requirement. Devise a solution before you enter this new phase of your life to ensure that you don't accidentally invite pests or unwanted attention to your tiny house.

Section 3: Tiny home dining solutions

Feeding yourself is also obviously important, no matter where you live. Human bodies require sustenance and creating an adequate nutritional experience when you have very little space to work within requires a smidge of creativity.

I like to think back to our ancestors, living in tiny dwellings or experiencing a nomadic lifestyle, much like the THOW. They spent all day hunting, gathering, farming, bartering, all for the purpose of survival. They followed their food sources, or they stayed put and made their own as farmers. Their dwellings didn't need a lot of space inside, because they didn't spend a lot of time inside. They didn't need a lot of room for food storage; instead, they immediately used every last scrap for practical purposes.

Today, we spend a woeful amount of time indoors and source most of our food from grocery stores and restaurants. But in a tiny house, there's one really big problem about shopping for groceries: Where are you going to put them?

Expansive gardens and tiny houses seem to go hand in hand, but there can be some complications. For example, where are you going to put your garden in your THOW? Sure, you can do some really cool things with containers, the rooftop, and even the bed of your pickup truck. Are you going to be able to grow everything you need in this scenario? Also, how will you store your fresh produce while you're on the road? You might plan to can extras for the cold season, but how are you going to do that in a tiny house, especially if you choose not to have electricity or running water. It's not impossible, but it will require a lot of forethought and research.

Regardless of where or how you structure your garden, it will need tending. Even the most wild garden will require occasional watering, weeding, seeding, and harvesting. In my experience, growing a vegetable and fruit garden is much easier than keeping an indoor houseplant, but the stakes are much higher. While a withered African violet is very sad, a shriveled up green bean vine or bush means no food.

If you are not experienced in gardening, you might want to try it out before you try to make homegrown products your main source of sustenance. Research what types of plants work well in your area, their sunlight and water requirements, and how to keep them healthy and happy. Find out what the yield is per seed or per plant, so you don't grow too much or too little of any particular crop. Don't forget to research common pests in your area also. I lost an entire crop of tomatoes to a very happy colony of moth larvae and donated my entire herb garden to the local deer. I may have lost food and money, but I gained a lot of knowledge with that particular planting season.

The benefits of gardening are plentiful, but then let's take it inside to the moment you need to store your wares. Do you have a refrigerator or a cooler? Are you going to be able to eat an entire piece of produce in one sitting? This may not be important when it comes to berries or beans, but what about larger produce, like melons, cabbages, or cucumbers. If you can't eat the whole thing, are you going to attempt to save the rest for another day or throw it back in the garden to become part of the circle of life?

The storage situation goes for things you don't produce as well. Shelf-stable foods are great as a backup or for use during the cooler months and can ensure that you have a well-rounded diet. But they also take up space. They generally like to be kept in cool, dry places, and pests absolutely love to dine upon them when you're not looking. Things like pasta, rice, and beans don't take up a lot of space, but you'll definitely want to transfer them into critter-proof containers, such as metal cans or thick plastic tubs.

In a regular-sized house, you might have a full set of durable leftover containers. After each meal, you rinse your plate and package the food that's left into a container that's just the right size and shape for your food before tucking it in the refrigerator. If you choose to include a refrigerator or cooler in your tiny home, this is still very possible and still a great idea.

However, how much room do you have for your reusable containers—both in the cupboards and in the cooler/refrigerator? You may want to keep a handful around for a variety of uses; after all, containers are always helpful for everything from leftover cabbage to broken crayons. This does mean, however, that you'll have to prioritize what you keep in your collection. Resealable bags and foil are great alternatives, but they do create extra waste to deal with. There really is no right or wrong answer for these dilemmas, but it's very important to consider them before you end up with a very expensive piece of cheese and nowhere to store it.

And finally, how about the actual prepping and cooking process? Cooking in a tiny house can not only be complicated but also downright dangerous, depending on what equipment and supplies you have.

Our tiny house includes a toaster, a microwave, a wood-burning stove, an outdoor firepit, and a grill. We also brought along our propane camping stove, which was part of our van setup. Our tiny house, on the other hand, is made of two-hundred-year-old reclaimed timber. We try very hard to do as much cooking outside as possible, simply out of respect for the structure and our safety.

You, on the other hand, may be perfectly comfortable with an indoor hibachi grill in your own tiny home. My first recommendation is that you ensure you have the right ventilation for your cooking methods, which may even be required by local building codes (yes, those again). I also recommend fire extinguishers, smoke alarms, and carbon monoxide detectors, as possible. Having worked in the insurance industry for long enough, a tiny house is very likely going to be a total loss in the event of a fire, but you can do your part to save the living beings just by having these three items handy at all times.

All risks aside, the food you buy should mirror the cooking methods you have available to you. If you only have a fire pit, it is highly unlikely that you will buy a vast array of TV dinners. You can find ways to boil water in a microwave, on a grill, or even on a wood burner, but that might not be conducive to making pasta or rice, depending on your set up. Don't buy anything you can't use or donate to a local food bank, or you'll have the potential for more mess, more waste, and more pests.

Food is a necessity, but feeding yourself in a tiny home can be a challenging experience, unless you're prepared for it. Gardens are a fun way to provide for yourself while reducing your carbon footprint, but a little extra elbow grease will be required. Additionally, you want to make sure you have a safe and critter-proof way of storing any shelf-stable foods. You may wish to employ a refrigerator or cooler to keep food fresher longer too.

Your fifty-piece coordinated mix-and-match reusable container set may not be able to make the tiny house transition with you, but that doesn't mean you can't keep anything at all. Explore the possibilities of having a few reusable containers around as well as eco-friendly options for bags and foil that won't drive up your waste.

Lastly, be mindful of the best way to feed your tiny household. You will need to do some experimentation to find out what works and what doesn't work, based on your lifestyle, house style, and environment. You don't necessarily have to minimize your meals, but you do want to be aware of the confines of your space and supplies.

Section 4: Tips for children and pets

When Brad and I first announced we were moving into a tiny house, the first question we got was usually, "Oh, you're both going to live there? At the same time?" As a result, I went into the experience very wary of how I might share the tiny space with another human being.

I cannot deny—and I don't think anyone who has ever lived in a small space can deny—that it comes with challenges. Having an upstairs and a downstairs helps, but if I need a moment to myself, I can only find it in the shower house or in the closet with the compost toilet. I have confirmed with people who live in double-loft tiny houses, double-bedroom tiny houses, and even condominiums that tread in tiny house territory that breathing room is at a premium when you share a tiny space with other carbon-based life forms.

Therefore, I have collected some thoughts from the tiny house community regarding sharing your space with children and pets. Perhaps this should be its own book, but I feel like I would need several decades of tiny house living and a doctorate in psychology to write that particular tome.

I have it on good authority from several mothers that your tiny house will never be free of minor messes when there are little ones about. You will step on crayons, LEGO bricks, doll arms, and tiny toy cars ... sometimes even if you don't own those items. Things will seem to break more easily because there are fewer places to keep them out of the way. Video games and devices with headphones are a very popular entertainment method because they are handheld and can be stored easily without requiring a lot of room.

However, no matter what you do, all the time will be family time. You will share breathing space at all times with your children. Every parent with whom I spoke recommended setting up a nook or area for the kids to have all to themselves, even if it's only during limited times. I've seen this frequently in van living as well. The kids will have their own bunk, which they can decorate to their own tastes and express themselves freely in that space. Regardless of what the space technically is, it's important for everyone in the household to have some "me space" and "me time."

In many instances, it's appropriate and recommended to expand your tiny household to include the outdoors. You can cook out there, you can work out there, and you can absolutely encourage your children to play out there. Many of the parents with whom I spoke indicated that they like to conduct homeschooling sessions outside as often as weather permits to ensure their kids get fresh air, sunshine, and the opportunity to explore the world.

Outdoor enrichment is one obvious solution to prevent children from feeling cooped up inside a tiny home, but what do you do when the weather doesn't cooperate? One mother explained to me that they like to use these days for visits to museums and science centers, whenever possible, but sometimes it's just a matter of sending each kid to their own space, and Mommy and Daddy do their best to get work done with a full house.

For every tip in this book, one father said to add the phrase, "and your kids, if you got 'em," meaning, for every tip included for your safety and sanity, apply that to the children as well. Every piece of furniture you want in the house, remember you need to provide the same for your children, including dining space, sitting/lounging space, and a sleeping area. Your water and power will be used by you ... and your kids, if you got 'em. You'll have your clothing and their clothing, your bathing supplies and theirs, books, computers, food, dining utensils, the greater collection of garbage ... everything will need a space.

Many THOW families have annexed their truck as a storage space, either with a cap on the bed or built-in bins and lockers. Given that modern trucks are chock-full of storage opportunities, this is a pretty resourceful idea. For those who are on a fixed foundation, consider throwing up a shed or outdoor storage closet for some gear. Either option can be a great place to put children's outdoor accessories, out-of-season clothing, or even surplus shelf-stable food to make as much use of the interior space as possible.

As I've never been a parent, I'll refrain from providing any in-depth parenting advice here for fear of treading into the deep unknown. However, I will say that every parent interviewed recommended keeping the kids outside and active as much as possible. Not only is it great for their development, mentally and physically, but it will keep everyone safe and sane when it comes to those indoor times.

With pets, the most common feedback I received was, "Oh the mess. You wouldn't believe the mess."

Consider all of the pet hair/feathers/droppings/trackings in your house. Now, consider all of the pet hair/feathers/droppings/trackings in your house if your entire living area was the size of your bedroom. If you try any of the experiments I recommended earlier, be sure to include your pet (and your kids, if you got 'em). Litter boxes, crates, terrariums, aquariums, cages, habitats … whatever environment your pet requires, make sure you are ok smelling, hearing, and seeing it at all times.

Bird owners have commented on dropped seeds growing into plants through their floorboards. Fish owners have mentioned that changing tanks in a tiny house is complicated, and sometimes, a fish will "go overboard" in a THOW. Small rodents often make a run for it, and while cats and dogs are often very helpful when it comes to pest control, they also shed uncontrollably, which means sweeping every crack and crevice several times a day.

You'll also need to consider disposing of pet waste, such as litterbox contents or habitat contents. You'll have more equipment and food to store as well. If you have a THOW, where will your pet ride during transit? How about veterinary care? Most states require rabies vaccinations for dogs and cats, so you'll need to stay on top of that, as well as scout out a local emergency vet while on the road.

Sharing your tiny house with a pet isn't impossible; it's just going to require a lot more thought and planning than keeping the same pet in a regular-sized dwelling. Just like children, you'll need to consider their overall enrichment as well as quality of life. Since pets cannot tell us what they like in words, we generally have to gauge their behaviors as a sign of their happiness.

Living in a tiny house with other individuals can be trying at times. Brad and I try our hardest to maintain separate levels of the house during the day since we both work from home. Each of us enjoys journeying outside to work in the fresh air, but bright sunlight and outdoor noises can complicate that at times. Creatively hanging a blanket or curtain in an area is one way to give yourself a little privacy from your spouse or children, but remember that your fortress is highly penetrable, and no solution can keep out all of the noise and activity.

Instead, embrace it for what it is, and look for opportunities to make your time together quality time. Use the resources you have at hand, such as the outdoors, to broaden both the tiny house experience and your space. Whether that means holding class outside, creating outdoor activities for the whole family, or getting really inventive with storage space for household goods, what you lack in interior space, you definitely make up for in ingenuity.

This chapter has likely brought some thoughts to the surface that you had never considered before. In my experience—and in that of other tiny house dwellers I've interviewed—these are all things that don't really manifest themselves in your consciousness until you cross the threshold for the first time. "Everything became real the moment I realized I couldn't bring my hair dryer," stated one friend, who moved to a historic working farmstead with a tiny rehabbed cabin. "I knew I wouldn't need my hair dryer on the farm, but it wasn't even an option."

There are a lot of things that are excluded from tiny house living, although your hair dryer may or may not be one of them. As you pack your belongings for donation or sale, as you consider how you're going to feed yourself, and as you wonder if Fluffy will truly be happy in your tiny house, remember: not everyone's experience is exactly the same.

At the same time, we all have what I now call "hair dryer moments." Like my friend, you'll discover something that simply doesn't work the same way in a tiny home. I absolutely miss my dishwasher, and I miss long hot baths with bath bombs. I know these are luxury items, and I'm lucky to have ever experienced them, but the truth is that we grow accustomed to a way of life, and when that lifestyle changes, we need to be prepared to change with it.

CONCLUSION

As I was writing this book, I kept puzzling over how I would conclude it. Unlike some of the other topics I've explored, this isn't a scenario where I can neatly say, "Well, that's how it's done, have fun!"

Tiny house living is an ever-evolving process for every individual. You become accustomed to waking up and sitting up carefully so you don't crack your noggin on the low ceiling. The sound of the solar panels rattling during a windstorm stops being alarming after a while, and you eventually learn to sleep through the sound of rain or hail pounding on a tin roof.

As the days go by, you stop feeling the need to turn on every light in the house. You find that you can just get by with that one light at the top of the stairs, especially if you work on the east side of the house in the morning and the west side of the house in the afternoon. You learn patterns that work, like keeping the furnace set at the bare minimum so it doesn't run out of power in the middle of a frigid night.

You may find you adapt faster than you imagined. You may discover that you have secretly been ready for this experience your entire life. If you've read through these pages and thought, *I already do that*, then you are far more prepared than many people are for the tiny house lifestyle.

You may also develop some strange habits as a result of your experiences. The glove box in my car is filled with napkins. Since I can't store them anywhere in my house, I impulsively pick them up and stuff them into my glove box. We use rags for cleaning, nose blowing, face wiping, and washing in our tiny house, so having something as luxurious as disposable paper ignites a hoarding instinct in me that I never knew existed.

I hope to have imparted the idea that your lifestyle dreams can come true. There are so many options available that, even when you're confronted with roadblocks, a little patience, research, and creativity can make a new path spring forth.

Hopefully, you'll have plenty of time to prepare for your tiny house transition. While patience is a virtue that many of us fail to practice, in this case, time is a very valuable asset. The more you plan ahead for your experience, the less shock and surprise you'll encounter once you start to get settled into your new home.

There will be plenty of decisions, choices, and ideas pushed onto your plate, and it will be overwhelming at times. Remember that notebook or journal I recommended at the beginning? In many cases, this will be your lifeline. You can fill it with every option, choice, or decision that comes your way. If you do have options written down in your journal, I recommend also noting what your final decision was, why you made it, and when you made it. This may sound like overkill, but it's really helpful to know what was on your mind when you're kicking yourself over a particular unforeseen consequence of your decision.

Tiny house living should be pleasant, but no lifestyle is without its challenges. My hope is that this book has prepared you for at least some of the upcoming process. It will no doubt be stressful, but hopefully it will be largely rewarding. After all, this is your dream, and you are permitted to let it come true to the best of your abilities.

I wish you all the best in your new tiny home. If you're on wheels, may your travels be swift and safe. If you're flying under the radar, may your discretion be your guide. And if you're working with a house full of children or pets, I wish you all serenity and a reliable broom.

With a little creativity, flexibility, and forethought, tiny house living can be exactly what you've always wanted it to be!

RESOURCES

I'd like to preface this section by stating that there are many resources out there for folks who are interested in tiny house living and construction. Much like van living, those in the community are frequently willing to share their stories and experiences, as well as tips and tricks for making it work. Much as we get excited to share "life hacks" online, tiny house dwellers really enjoy finding ways to make their lives easier and more productive, even within the self-imposed limits of a tiny home.

Therefore, I want to say that there really are no bad resources when it comes to learning more about tiny house living. Every point of view is going to be slightly different. Some articles will leave you wanting more information, while others may take a few days to peruse and digest the abundance of detailed information provided. After all, if there's one key takeaway in this book, it should be that building and enjoying your tiny home is a deeply personal experience that deserves serious deliberation.

So please consider these resources simply as a way to get started. I'm not personally affiliated with any of these sites, and I'm not specifically endorsing them. I simply felt that the information contained on these sites is fantastic for getting your feet wet and for providing a variety of perspectives on tiny home living.

Read on and be sure to vet the information you glean from these sites with your own needs and experiences. Remember, even if you're isolated in a tiny house, you're never alone, thanks to the vast online community of tiny house dwellers willing to lend some thoughts, advice, and warm words to you!

Knowledge Base | FAQs

The folks at Tiny Home Builders have provided many online resources on their site, which can be used as stand-alone reference guides or an overall encyclopedia of tiny house information.

This link leads to their Knowledge Base, which is essentially an FAQ about everything tiny house related. Again, I don't know these folks, nor is this an endorsement for their site or products, but the ideas and information reflected in this knowledge base provides a very well-rounded guide to some of the most common questions you'll have about tiny house living—and even some questions you haven't thought of yet.

I placed this link first in the Resources because it's vastly comprehensive, which makes it an excellent place to start and return to time and again.

Tiny House Knowledge Base
https://www.tinyhomebuilders.com/tiny-house-knowledge-base

General Assistance

The following links lead to sites that have a lot of general information about tiny house living. I've included a few different points of view so that you can gauge the similarities and differences for yourself. Each site or blog is compiled by actual tiny home dwellers and can provide you with intimate insights that you otherwise won't appreciate until you've spent some time in your own tiny house.

Tiny Home Builders Help Sites
https://www.tinyhomebuilders.com/help/tiny-house-movement
https://www.tinyhomebuilders.com/blog/tiny-house-questions/

The Tiny House Movement Blog
https://www.rockethomes.com/blog/home-buying/tiny-house

Living Big in a Tiny House
Bryce Langston and Rasa Pescud are based in New Zealand and provide an international outlook to various types of tiny house living. They've started a YouTube channel in which they interview other tiny home dwellers and experience many different tiny house lifestyles. This is a fun resource if you really want to get an idea of how amazingly customized the tiny house experience can be.
https://www.livingbiginatinyhouse.com/tiny-house/
https://www.youtube.com/user/livingbigtinyhouse

Tiny House Construction
As you're aware, this is not a book about tiny house construction. However, you're likely looking for a few resources to get you started in the process of understanding and appreciating various tiny house layouts. The following links provide more in-depth information on the topics of types of tiny houses, building code considerations, as well as details about towing and stowing your tiny house on wheels.

Types of Tiny House
https://www.tinyhouse.com/post/7-types-of-tiny-homes
https://www.tinysociety.co/articles/11-beautiful-types-of-tiny-houses/
https://cozeliving.com/beginners-guide-different-types-of-tiny-houses/

Examples of Tiny House Floor Plans
As stated earlier, this is not an endorsement or recommendation, so always be sure to fully research and vet any house plans that you choose to pur-

chase online. Make sure the project is within your scope, affordable, and will meet your local building code requirements.

https://www.houseplans.com/collection/tiny-house-plans

https://tinyhouseplans.com/

Building Codes

Speaking of building codes, here are some links that lead to information on the topic. I cannot vouch for how accurate all of the details are via each link in the future, but at the time of publication, they did correctly lead to accurate details.

2018 International Residential Code (IRC)

https://codes.iccsafe.org/content/IRC2018/appendix-q-tiny-houses

Interpretation of 2018 IRC

https://buildingcodetrainer.com/building-codes-for-a-tiny-house/

State By State Tiny House Laws and Regulations - Scroll down to link to each state individually.

https://www.moneytaskforce.com/real-estate/tiny-house-laws-state-regulations/

Towing and parking your Tiny House On Wheels

https://www.tinyhomebuilders.com/help/tiny-house-towing-guide

https://www.tinyhomebuilders.com/help/tiny-house-parking-guide

Truck Recommendations

https://www.motorbiscuit.com/trucks-tow-small-house/

Dimension Recommendations

https://www.supertinyhomes.com/tiny-houses/weight-size-without-permit.html

Costs and other Financial Considerations

https://www.tinyhomebuilders.com/tiny-houses/build-your-house

https://www.tinyhomebuilders.com/blog/tiny-house-cost/

https://www.mortgages.com/buying-house-and-owning-home/pros-and-cons-owning-tiny-home

Interior Aspects

Just as there are plenty of things to consider when building and towing your tiny home, you'll need to know the latest and greatest updates regarding the interior. The following links provide tips and tricks for creating, installing, and maintaining the various rooms in your tiny house. While not every layout will work for every house or person living in it, these links provide some interesting ideas and insight to help you prepare for the idea of a tiny bathroom, tiny kitchen, and minimized living area.

Bathrooms

https://www.thespruce.com/tiny-showers-4156387

https://www.supertinyhomes.com/tiny-houses/bathroom.html

https://thetinylife.com/designing-your-dream-tiny-house-bathroom-advice-from-a-full-time-tiny-houser/

Kitchen

https://www.tinyhomebuilders.com/blog/tiny-house-kitchen-design/

https://www.homestratosphere.com/tiny-house-kitchen-ideas/

https://tinyhousehugeideas.com/small-kitchen-ideas/

Furniture Ideas

https://www.livingbiginatinyhouse.com/articles/top-transforming-and-multifunctional-furniture-ideas-for-tiny-homes/

https://www.godownsize.com/tiny-house-furniture-small-space/

Power and Utilities

Again, this is not intended to be a building or construction guidebook, but I do feel that knowledge is power. Before you make any hard and final decisions regarding utilities in your tiny house, here are some resources to help you understand the function, cost, and process to make these things work.

Wiring Details

https://bbtinyhouses.com/how-do-i-get-power-water-to-my-tiny-house-all-about-tiny-house-hookups/

https://tinylivinglife.com/2019/05/how-to-power-a-tiny-home/

The Pros and Cons of Solar Power

The blog post from Thetinyhouse.net is particularly interesting, as it provides two points of view regarding the pros and cons of using solar panels for your power source.

https://www.thetinyhouse.net/solar-powered-tiny-house/

https://thetinylife.com/tiny-house-solar/

Water and Sewage

https://www.supertinyhomes.com/tiny-houses/water.html

https://tinyhouseexpedition.com/the-different-tiny-house-plumbing-options-you-should-know/

More Details on Organization Styles and Options

If you're scared, concerned, intimidated, or stressed out about the transition from a regular sized house into a tiny home, you're not alone. These are some resources to provide you with extra information and guidance regarding some of the organization and minimization tips and tricks mentioned in the book.

While this is true of all of the posted links, I'd like to point out that while the link takes you directly to a page that I feel is a decent resource for each topic, feel free to explore each blog, webpage, or resource in detail. These lifestyle sites provide a wealth of information on a variety of topics, not just getting your tiny house organized!

Capsule Wardrobes/Lifestyle

https://www.amazon.com/Capsule-Craze-Rebecca-Elligton/dp/1735025356/ref=tmm_pap_swatch_0?_encoding=UTF8&qid=1620232576&sr=8-8

https://goodonyou.eco/capsule-wardrobes-create-your-own/

Minimalism

https://www.moneyunder30.com/minimalist-living

https://www.becomingminimalist.com/what-is-minimalism/

https://www.theminimalists.com/minimalism/

Other Methods of De-Cluttering and Streamlining

https://www.lifehack.org/articles/productivity/how-organize-your-life-10-habits-really-organized-people.html

https://www.clutterkeeper.com/organize-tiny-house/

https://thetinylife.com/tiny-house-storage/

Experiences & Blogs

There are quite literally hundreds of tiny house bloggers out there, and I can't possibly name them all. Here are a few that provide a wealth of information on everything from how to make your bed in a tiny house to following folks on their journey into tiny house living.

The last link is a blog round up. I will confess that I'm not familiar with every blog on this list as the site is updated frequently.

https://tinyhousegiantjourney.com/
https://tinyhouseblog.com/
https://thetinylife.com/
https://tinyhousecommunity.com/
https://blog.feedspot.com/tiny_house_blogs/

Communities

As is the case with everything in this Resources section, I don't want to appear to be specifically promoting or favoring one group or resource over another. There are so many tiny house communities online for different niches and preferences that I feel like I can't possibly do them all justice. The following links should get you started, however.

Whatever social media outlet you prefer, Facebook, Instagram, Twitter, Reddit, Tumblr, and even LinkedIn have resources and groups for those interested in and participating in the tiny house lifestyle.

https://www.facebook.com/TinyHouseCommunity/
https://www.thetinyhouse.net/find-local-tiny-house-communities/
https://tinyhouseblog.com/tiny-house/tiny-house-friends-world-just-go-meet/
https://unitedtinyhouse.com/

The best part of any adventure is the special memories you make along the way!

This travel journal will provide you full access to chronicling your journey and adventures through van life. Go to **https://www.kristine-hudson.com/vanlife** to download it for free.

Reviews

Reviews and feedback help improve this book and the author. If you enjoy this book, we would greatly appreciate it if you could take a few moments to share your opinion and post a review on Amazon.

Also by Kristine Hudson

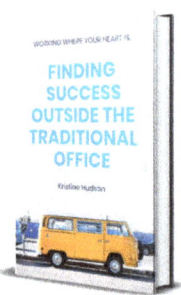

Finding Success Outside The Traditional Office

mybook.to/workfromanywhere

How to Choose the Ultimate Side-hustle

mybook.to/side-hustle

From Wheels to Wellness

mybook.to/Healthinvan

www.ingramcontent.com/pod-product-compliance
Lightning Source LLC
Chambersburg PA
CBHW071413070526
44578CB00003B/564